ESSENTIAL
SHRUBS

ESSENTIAL
SHRUBS
The 100 Best for Design and Cultivation

Text by Peggy Fisher • Photography by Derek Fell

CRESCENT BOOKS
NEW YORK

A FRIEDMAN GROUP BOOK

This 1990 edition published by Crescent Books
distributed by Crown Publishers, Inc.
225 Park Avenue South
New York, New York 10003

LIBRARY OF CONGRESS CATALOGING-IN-PUBLICATION DATA

Fischer, Peggy.
   Essential shrubs / by Peggy Fischer.
      p.   cm.
   ISBN 0-517-67661-3
   1. Ornamental shrubs. 2. Ornamental shrubs—Pictorial works.
3. Landscape gardening.   I. Title.
SB434.F556   1989
635.9′76—dc20   89-27407
                                                                                CIP

ESSENTIAL SHRUBS: The 100 Best for Design and Cultivation
was prepared and produced by
Michael Friedman Publishing Group, Inc.
15 West 26th Street
New York, New York 10010

Editor: Sharon Kalman
Art Director: Robert W. Kosturko
Layout: Deborah Kaplan
Photo Editor: Christopher Bain
Production Manager: Karen L. Greenberg

Typeset by: Mar+X Myles Graphics, Inc.
Color Separation by: United South Sea Graphic Art Co., Ltd.
Printed and bound in Hong Kong by South China Printing Co.(1988) Limited

h g f e d c b a

DEDICATION

To my mother and Phyllis.

ACKNOWLEDGMENTS

Derek Fell wishes to thank the many garden owners who kindly allowed him access to their beautiful tree and shrub plantings, especially Hiroshi Makita, garden designer; Ruth Levitan, Stamford Connecticut; and H. Thomas Hallowell Jr., whose Deerfield Garden near Rydel, Pennsylvania contains some of the finest tree and shrub plantings in North America.

TABLE OF CONTENTS

INTRODUCTION

COLORFUL, LONG-LIVED PLANTS FOR LITTLE EFFORT

CONTRARY TO POPULAR BELIEF, THE OLDEST life forms on earth are not trees—not the giant redwoods of coastal California or the ancient bristlecone pine of the Rocky Mountains. The appearance of certain shrubs preceded trees by at least 3,000 years. In California's Sonora Desert, a creosote bush nicknamed 'King Clone' is believed to be over 10,000 years old; in Western Pennsylvania, a box huckleberry is believed to be 13,000 years old. Over the centuries, this plant has established itself across many acres in an ever-spreading clump, which began from a seedling.

Shrubs, known as "woody plants", are a large, long-lived group of plants that includes trees, shrubs, and subshrubs. By definition, a shrub is any woody plant that has multiple stems rising from the ground. True shrubs differ from trees in that they have multi-stems or multiple trunks emerging from the soil, and generally remain below 15 feet in height. Trees tend to grow a single, main trunk, and are capable of growing to more than 15 feet. Subshrubs are a group of plants normally considered to be perennials that develop wood parts with age. Examples of subshrubs include candytuft, lavender, and rosemary.

These broad definitions are not clear-cut since there are too many exceptions to establish any rules. For example, if cut to the ground, many trees will sprout multiple stems around the damaged trunk, becoming shrublike. Similarly, even true shrubs and subshrubs, given ideal conditions, can be trained to a single stem and can grow to 15 feet.

CLASSIFYING SHRUBS

The three classifications of woody plants—trees, shrubs, and subshrubs—serve different purposes in the landscape.

Shrubs provide decoration at eye level. If these have beautiful flowers or attractive berries they are generally referred to as flowering shrubs, and are used like other flowering plants to provide eye-catching color. Subshrubs are low-growing plants that provide interest at ground level. They are used most commonly in perennial borders. Apart from their flow-

ering effect, shrubs make good hedges, carefree ground covers, and wall-covering vines. Even if they have inconspicuous flowers, decorative leaves often make shrubs worth planting as camouflage for monotonous expanses of wall or fencing. Some shrubs can take the form of trees, while some trees can take the form of a shrub.

Besides planting shrubs for the shape, texture, and color of their leaves, they can be either *deciduous* or *evergreen*. Deciduous shrubs drop their leaves in autumn, sometimes preceded by dramatic fall coloring. Evergreens, which retain their leaves throughout the year, are further classified as narrowleaf evergreens—such as pines—and broadleaf evergreens— such as rhododendrons and hollies.

The fall color of many deciduous shrubs is often dramatic enough to outshine the beauty of flowers. Burning bush (*Euonymus alata*) and many Japanese maples (*Acer japonicum*) have scarlet leaves in fall as red as many azalea flowers. These and other shrubs also have interesting wintry silhouettes, especially when seen against a background of white.

Evergreens can help to form the framework of a landscape design. Plants such as boxwood and yew can form corridors to guide the eye from one space to another; they can form boundaries, outline garden spaces, and define planting beds for flowering plants. And, their growth can be pruned into vertical accents such as cones, spheres, and mounds.

Many shrubs—whether evergreen or deciduous—can be trained to create special decorative effects, such as bonsai—the art of pruning and restricting the roots of shrubs to create miniature forms; espalier—the art of training shrubs to form patterns against a wall or fence; and topiary—the art of pruning shrubs into shapes such as animal and human forms.

Shrubs suitable as hedges can be planted to make screens for privacy, as well as for parterres—low hedges forming patterns and planting spaces—and mazes—intricate passages that challenge people to find their way into the middle and out again; and as windbreaks to cushion the force of wind and salt spray.

Considering the years of satisfaction shrubs can give, it is worth taking the time to choose the right shrubs for your needs, and to understand their needs, including what type of soil they grow best in, whether or not they need sun or can bear wind or salt sprays, and how and when to prune.

Opposite page, top: Japanese cut-leaf maples not only have a pleasing shape, but also spectacular fall coloring.

Opposite page, bottom: Billowing forms of evergreen azalea and rhododendron overhung with spreading branches of deciduous dogwood combine to create a spectacular winter scene.

Left: Here yew, pruned to a cone shape, contrasts with myrtle growing in a planter box and pruned to a "pom-pon" shape.

CHAPTER ONE

CARING FOR SHRUBS

BEFORE PLANTING

THERE ARE SOME FUNDAMENTAL STEPS THAT need to be considered even before you place a shrub in the ground.

Where and What To Buy

The most convenient place to buy shrubs is from a garden center or nursery located close to your home. On display they are likely to have plants offered in different ways at different price levels. For example, most shrubs are sold "bare-root". Deciduous and evergreen shrubs are dug from the field when dormant. The soil is washed from them, and the roots are wrapped in moist sphagnum moss and enclosed in plastic. Bare-root plants should be purchased and planted in the fall or spring while the plants are still dormant. Prices for bare-root stock tend to be the most economical.

At the next price level are shrubs sold in containers, which can be made of plastic, wood, metal, or fiber. The plants can be slipped out of their containers—usually a one gallon capacity—and planted with large root balls. There is minimal root disturbance and the transplant success rate is high.

At the next price level are shrubs that are "balled and burlapped." These have been dug from the fields by a special machine that picks up a large, round root mass and wraps it in burlap. This technique enables extra large specimens and evergreens to survive transplanting. Prices for balled and burlapped plants are higher than bare-root plants.

Mail-order nurseries provide another source for shrubs. They tend to offer a far wider selection than do garden centers, including rare plants. Also, some catalogs specialize in a particular family of shrubs—such as roses and rhododendrons. A list of the most important mail order houses are found in the back of this book, page 124.

Almost all mail-order shrubs are sent bare-root. It is important to open your mail order shipment immediately and examine the roots and top growth for signs of damage. If there are any broken roots or stems of a superficial nature, just prune them away before planting. However, if the main support branches are broken, if a tap root is snapped in two, or if there are signs of rodent damage—where the bark at the soil line has been nibbled away in a complete circle—the shipment should be returned for replacement or refund. For information on planting bare-root shrubs see page 15.

Choosing a Site

You must decide whether your planting site is to be in the sun or shade, and whether the drainage of your site is good or poor. It is hard to provide shade for a sunny site, but a shady site can often be improved by simply removing overhanging branches from trees. The choice of shrubs available for planting in the sun is far greater than the choice available for shade.

Poor drainage will severely restrict your choice of plants. However, a poorly drained site can be easily improved by "berming"—mounding top soil over the poorly drained area—or by building a raised bed of landscape ties with top soil dumped in the middle.

If high winds or salt spray are a problem, a shelter of wind-resistant or salt-tolerant windbreak plants can be established on the side exposed to prevailing winds. To establish a windbreak it may be necessary to protect the young plants until they are well-established (a year or two) by erecting a temporary screen using hay bales to form a wall, or rolls of burlap to form a fence.

Soil Conditions

Though many shrubs will survive in poor, infertile soil, best results are achieved by determining the nature of your soil and how to improve it. Poor soil can be classified as sandy or clay. Sandy soil has little moisture or nutrient-holding capacity. Though plant roots can penetrate sand freely, they starve from lack of moisture and nutrients. Soil with a lot of clay is heavy, sticky, and cold, creating an impenetrable barrier for plant roots. The "happy medium" is loam soil. It is not too light, or too heavy, it is porous enough to allow excess water to drain away, yet holds moisture and nutrients for feeding roots continuously. The remedy for sandy and clay soil is the addition of humus. By adding humus (composed of decomposed organic matter), sand becomes moisture- and nutrient-retentive and clay becomes aerated with fibers and particles allowing roots freedom to roam.

Soils also can be acidic or alkaline in their chemical balance. The amount of acidity or alkalinity is measured by the pH scale. A rating of seven is neutral—anything above seven is alkaline and below is acidic. Some plants, such as azaleas and hollies, demand a low pH content (acid). Acidity can be reduced by adding lime; alkalinity can be reduced by adding sulphur peat or leaf mold to soil.

Acidic soils generally persist in forested areas with high rainfall. Alkaline soils prevail in areas with low rainfall, such as desert regions. A soil test conducted through a soil laboratory (check your county extension service for the address of the nearest extention) will tell you the nature of your soil and also recommend specific nutrients and soil conditioners for improvement.

PLANTING

Specific planting instructions for shrubs depend mostly on the type of transplant purchased: bare-root, containered, or balled and burlapped.

Bare-Root If the soil is in good condition, composed of fairly loose loam, simply dig a hole deep enough to accommodate the deepest roots. Center the plant in the hole and put the soil back, making sure the roots are splayed out as much as possible, and there is good soil contact. Water and tamp down the soil with your foot, adding more soil to level off any major settling. A slight depression around the rim to help catch rainwater is advisable. Cover the base of the plant with a mulch of wood chips or shredded leaves. Fertilize by sprinkling granular fertilizer over the surrounding soil surface, and again each year in spring.

Containered Plants Try to remove containered plants with as little root disturbance as possible. Fiber containers can be torn open to help slide the root ball out. With tough plastic or metal containers you may need to slide a long-bladed knife around the rim first to loosen the root ball. In good loam soil simply dig a hole slightly larger in size than the root ball and ensure a snug fit by filling the edges with excavated soil.

Leave a slight depression to catch rainwater and place a layer of wood chips or shredded leaves around the plant. Fertilizing can be done by lightly sprinkling a general purpose fertilizer over the soil surface.

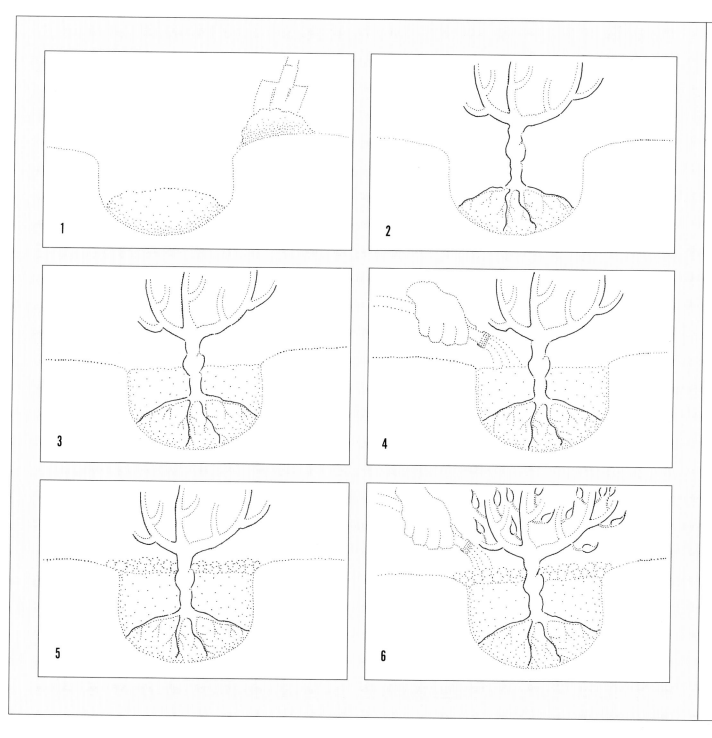

PLANTING A BARE-ROOT SHRUB

1-Dig a hole deep enough and wide enough to accommodate the roots. Mound the bottom with top soil.

2-Position the shrub in the center of the hole so the roots are splayed out and around the mound.

3-Fill the hole to within 1 inch of the rim.

4-Water and tamp the soil down. Add more soil to compensate for any settling.

5-Lay organic mulch over the hole.

6-Water whenever the soil feels dry.

HOW TO PLANT A SHRUB

For the purpose of showing the proper planting of a shrub, we have chosen a rhododendron which has been balled in burlap sacking. (For planting a bare-root shrub, see diagram on page 15.)

1. At the garden center, examine your proposed purchase for healthy green leaves and any signs of bark damage by mice; also check for insect infestations, such as scale and spider mites.

2. Rest the plant on the ground. The string holding the burlap in place must be removed prior to planting.

3. Dig a hole to the depth of the root ball and slightly wider than its diameter. This soil was enriched with compost and peat moss to make it sufficiently moist and acid for a rhododendron.

4. Gently loosen the burlap and use it to maneuver the root ball into the hole. The burlap does not need to be removed completely.

5. Fill the hole and apply a layer of loose organic material, such as a mulch, around the base of the plant to deter weeds and conserve moisture. Pine needles are the mulch material used here.

6. Water thoroughly—at least once a week in the absence of natural rainfall.

7. The newly planted rhododendron looks comfortable in its new home.

8. Within ten days of planting, the rhododendron (variety Vulcan) is flowering profusely.

Balled & Burlapped

These can be extremely heavy and awkward to move because of the size of the root ball. Use a sturdy wheelbarrow to move heavy specimens to the planting site, and enlist help in lifting it into the hole, which should be slightly wider and slightly deeper than the root ball. Loosen any string or wire, remove nails, and unwrap the top of the burlap from around the stems. Do not remove the burlap completely, otherwise the root ball is likely to fall apart and leave you with little more than a bare-root plant. Once the burlap sack is moistened with water and in contact with the soil it soon decomposes. Leave a slight depression around the plant to help catch rainwater, and mulch with wood chips or shredded leaves. If any fertilizer is needed, just sprinkle it lightly in granular form over the soil surface all around the plant extending to slightly beyond the drip line.

AFTER CARE

The following instructions apply after the shrub is comfortably seated in its planting hole.

Staking Unless shrubs are unusually tall they generally do not need staking to keep them upright. However, if staking is needed, use wire or strong string like guy ropes. Be sure to cushion the part of the plant that comes into contact with the string with pieces of folded cloth.

Watering The biggest cause of failure with new shrubs is dehydration, either because the plants were not sufficiently watered to begin with, or because they received insufficient amounts of water after they were planted. After planting, water thoroughly. In the event of a week without natural rainfall, try to give newly planted shrubs at least three gallons of water per plant per week.

Winter Protection Newly planted shrubs—especially those planted in autumn—are susceptible to winter-kill from cold winds that dehydrate bare limbs. In exposed locations, shield valuable new plantings with a burlap screen; mulch plants after the ground has frozen, and keep snow off limbs before the snow has a chance to freeze. Hardy shrubs have

roots that can survive freezing by going dormant, but damage can occur when an early thaw breaks dormancy, followed by a freeze that kills the vulnerable roots. A mulch applied after the ground freezes helps keep the ground frozen until a sustained thaw sets in. Where shrubs are positioned under the eaves of a house—as in foundation plantings—they should be covered with wooden structures that can break the fall of snow from the roof pitch.

Fertilizing Shrubs benefit from an annual application of fertilizer, particularly a well-balanced fertilizer that provides adequate amounts of nitrogen (to stimulate leafy growth), phosphorus (to stimulate flowering and root development), and potassium (for disease resistance). You can tell whether a fertilizer has a balance of these nutrients by the set of three numbers printed on the label, such as 10-10-10 or 20-20-

Opposite page: This Japanese cut-leaf maple shows its ornamental value even in winter, as light snowfall accentuates its billowing form and cascading tracery of branches.

Left: A balance between deciduous trees and evergreens in this woodland garden creates a spectacular composition in the fall.

Right, top: High hedges demand special pruning techniques to keep them shapely. Here, an electric hedge trimmer is used for speed. A stepladder laid between two 'A-frame' ladders has a plank laid over the rungs to make a "cat-walk," providing a firm walking surface.

Right, bottom: Severe pruning of evergreen shrubs, such as lilacs, makes them bushy.

20, meaning each has equal percentages of the three major nutrients, known as NPK for nitrogen, phosphorus, and potassium, in that order.

A light surface feeding of a granular fertilizer at the time you plant and then a regular surface feeding each spring at recommended rates should keep shrubs vigorous and healthy. Make sure that the surface area covered extends slightly beyond the drip line (the area where rain would drip from the leaves around the periphery of the plant) to encourage roots to reach out beyond the growing perimeter. Do not put fertilizer directly into planting holes because the roots may be burned from an overdose. It is not necessary to drill holes deep into the soil for shrub fertilizers to work. Tests have proven that simple surface feeding (except on slopes) is more effective since most feeder roots are close to the soil surface.

Pruning

Once a shrub is established, several ways of pruning should be considered to keep it healthy and attractive. Following are different kinds of pruning techniques and the tools needed:

Shearing This is done to shape a plant to a particular contour—a box shape in the case of a hedge, but also a mound, globe, cone, or column, and even more fanciful shapes like topiary animals. Shearing cuts encourage bushy growth where the cut is made. Shearing is done primarily with a pair of hand pruning shears or by an electric hedge trimmer, which is considerably faster.

Thinning This consists of selectively removing excess branches—especially dead branches—to open up the plant for better air circulation. Thinning cuts should be made at ground level; they do not make the plant bushier. Thinning can be done with scimitar hand pruners for branches up to 1/4-inch thickness, or with a pruning saw for easily reached thicker branches. To cut thick branches that are difficult to reach, a long handled "lopper" works well. Thinning is especially effective for encouraging generous berry clusters and fruit yields.

Rejuvenation (or "Take it to the ground" pruning) Many old shrubs need drastic pruning. When plants like for-

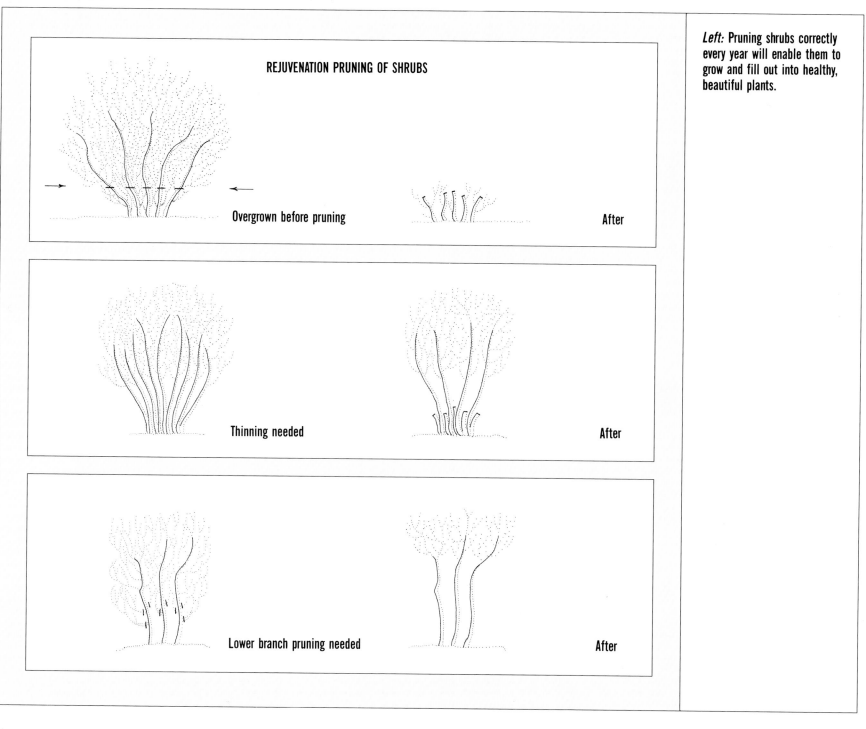

REJUVENATION PRUNING OF SHRUBS

Overgrown before pruning

After

Thinning needed

After

Lower branch pruning needed

After

Left: Pruning shrubs correctly every year will enable them to grow and fill out into healthy, beautiful plants.

Right: There are many common shrub shapes that can be achieved by pruning. Some of the most popular are illustrated here.

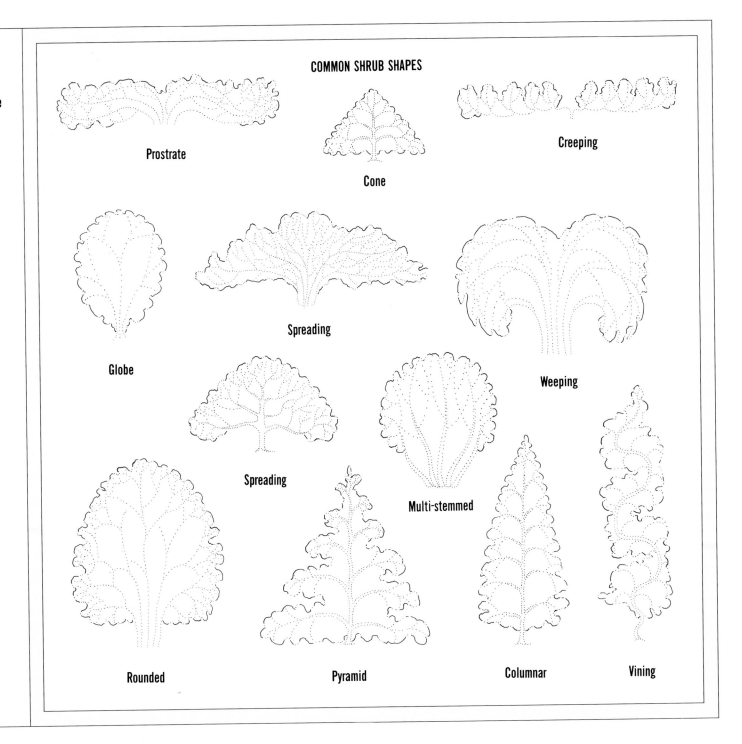

COMMON SHRUB SHAPES

Prostrate

Cone

Creeping

Globe

Spreading

Weeping

Spreading

Multi-stemmed

Rounded

Pyramid

Columnar

Vining

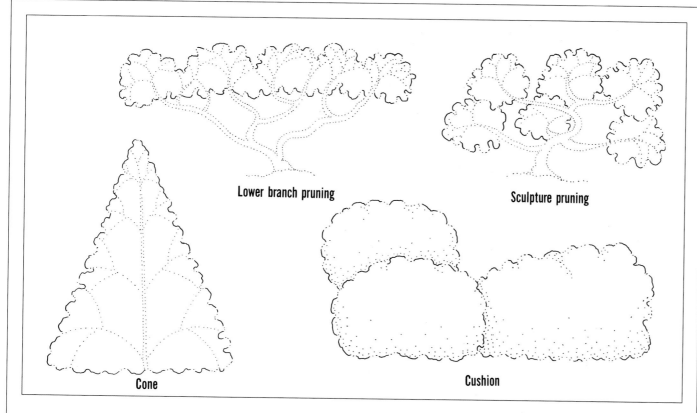

Lower branch pruning

Sculpture pruning

Cone

Cushion

sythia, lilac, and viburnum become overgrown and untidy, they can be cut to within 6 inches of the ground either with a lopper or a swipe of the chain saw. This encourages the plant to send up a host of new shoots that can be shaped as desired.

Weed Control Though some shrubs will grow through turf, it is always best to keep the area encompassing the drip line clear of sod or competition from weeds. A layer of organic material placed around the plant will help suffocate weeds. The very best mulch materials are shredded leaves or shredded bark. Bark chips and wood chips are not as desirable since they are known to attract a fungus that can attack the roots of shrubs.

Shrub Shapes Shrubs are extremely versatile in their growth habit, allowing for many useful functions in the landscape. Below are some basic shapes, along with some design ideas, for low-spreading shrubs suitable as ground covers, to

tall, rambling vines for covering walls and arbors.

Prostrate. Example: *Juniperus horizontalis*, 'Blue Rug Juniper.' Excellent for ground cover and erosion control.

Low-spreading. Example: *Skimmia japonica*, 'Skimmia.' Excellent in rock gardens and low beds.

Weeping. Example: *Spiraea* species, 'Spiraea.' Excellent lawn accent.

Pyramid. Example: *Picea pungens nana*, 'Dwarf Blue Spruce.' Excellent lawn accent.

Columnar. Example: *Taxus cuspidata*, 'Upright Yew.' Excellent for vertical accents and tall hedges.

Globular. Example: *Buxus sempervirens*, 'Boxwood.' Excellent for edging walkways, and for hedges.

Vine. Example: *Wisteria floribunda*, 'Wisteria.' Good to cover walls and arbors.

Mounded. Example: *Hydrangea macrophylla*, 'Hydrangea.' Good lawn accent, foundation highlight, and hedge.

Right, top: The Exbury azalea, 'Golden Sunset', planted along a stream bank.

Right, bottom: The tall, cone-shaped form of an Alberta spruce adds a vertical accent to this shrub border.

STARTING SHRUBS FROM SEEDS

1. Materials needed are: peat or plastic trays and pots, packets of seed, and planter mix of equal parts peat, sand, and vermiculite, or purchase a brand-name starter mix.

2. Press moist planter mix into container. The mixture should be sufficiently moist so that when squeezed tightly a few water drops will appear.

3. Sow seed evenly on the surface. The seed packet will specify the recommended depth depending on size.

4. Cover large seeds with a layer of planting mix. Leave fine seeds uncovered, since they generally need light to germinate.

PROPAGATION

Although it's a lot easier to buy ready-grown plants from a nursery or mail-order house, shrubs can be grown inexpensively using a variety of propagating techniques. The process may sometimes be tedious, but the sense of accomplishment gained by raising a beautiful specimen from seed or cuttings can be immensely uplifting. The following techniques are within the capability of most gardeners.

Seeds Though some shrubs are sterile through hybridizing, and do not set viable seed, the vast majority produce large quantities of seed, varying in size from grains of pepper to bean-size. Some are easy to germinate, others have special needs. One interesting aspect involving shrub seeds is that you can never be certain of growing a plant identical to the one from which the seed came. The seedlings can be highly variable in both color and habit. (To be assured of an identical match, you should take cuttings from the shrub.) Some good shrubs to experiment with starting from seed include the hardy-orange (*Poncirus trifoliata*), the trumpet-vine (*Campsis radicans*), and camellias (*Camellia japonica*). These plants are relatively easy to germinate using fresh seeds.

Start the seeds on a tray of flats filled with potting soil composed of equal parts of sand and peat moss. Cover the seeds with about 1 inch of potting soil (smaller seeds need less coverage).

Cover the tray with glass to establish a humid environment, maintaining a soil temperature of about 70°F (this can be done with a heating cable). Once seeds germinate remove the glass cover. Keep the soil moist and in bright light, but out of direct sunlight. A cold frame in a partially shaded area is an ideal place for raising seedlings. Transplant seedlings to individual containers once they are large enough to handle.

Cuttings Many shrubs are easy to root from cuttings. In fact, some will often sprout roots simply by being inserted in water: for example, Forsythia and Pussy Willow. Other shrubs, like Roses, Lilacs, and Honeysuckle will root quite quickly (within several weeks) in a moist potting soil. Slow-growing plants like hollies and magnolias generally take a long time to form roots—up to three months. Some shrubs

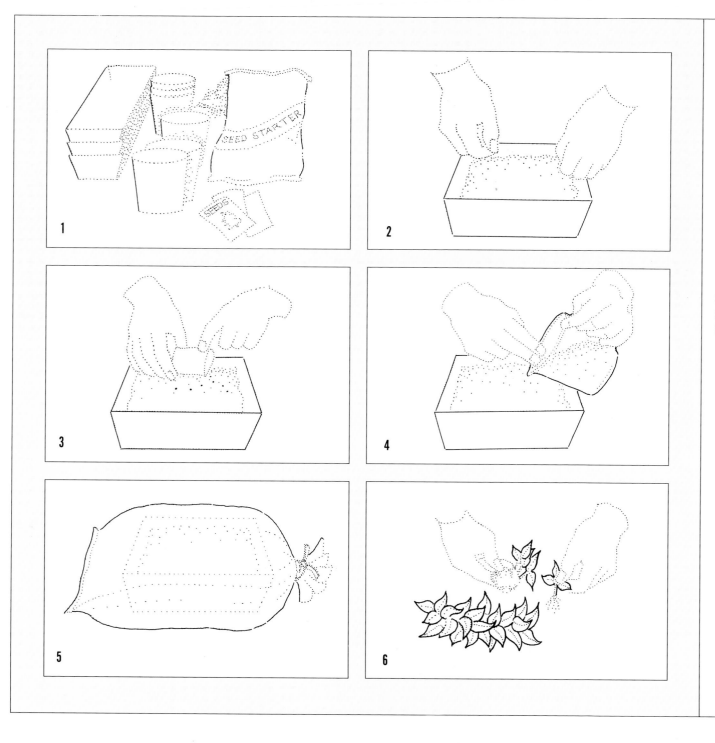

5. Place the container in a polyethylene bag (a kitchen freezer bag), close the end and keep in a warm place (about 70°F) until the seeds germinate. A freezer bag creates a self-contained micro-climate, so leave the container alone until the seeds germinate.

6. When the seeds have germinated, remove the freezer bag and begin watering and fertilizing seedlings with liquid plant food. When they are large enough to handle, separate and transfer them to individual pots.

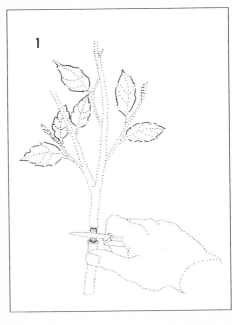

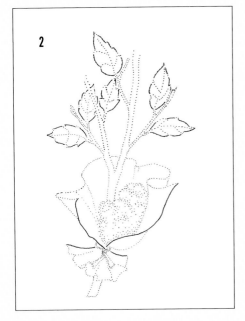

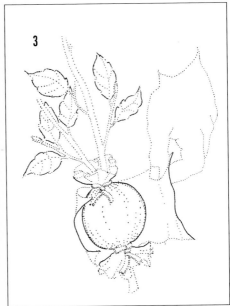

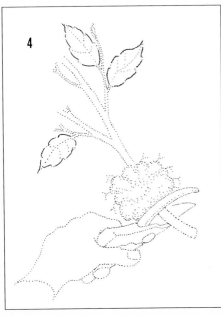

root best when cuttings are taken of new soft growth in spring, others from mature wood in autumn, referred to as hard wood cuttings. For a complete list of shrubs suitable for taking cuttings, see lists on page 112-113.

Cuttings are usually 4- to 6-inch sections of stem taken from the branch tips. Do this by cutting the ends on a diagonal and removing the lower leaves. Slit the cut end lengthwise, just enough to expose the inner wood. Once this is done, dip the cut ends in a rooting hormone and stick them upright into a pot or tray of moist starting soil containing equal parts sand, peat, and perlite. Enclose the container of cuttings with a clear plastic bag to create a humid microclimate. Keep the cuttings at room temperature in low light. Kept in moist soil, the cuttings should be well-rooted in 3 to 12 weeks, depending on variety, after which they can be transferred to individual pots until they are large enough to be transplanted into the garden. Easy shrubs to start from cuttings include pussy willows (*Salix discolor*), Gold-dust shrub (*Aucuba japonica*), and Red-twig dogwood (*Cornus sericea*). If cuttings are started outdoors in a cold frame or specially prepared nursery bed, they should be protected from the direct rays of sun with shade cloth. Regular watering is essential since a cutting without an established root system can dehydrate quickly unless protected by shade and given a daily watering during dry spells.

Soil Layering The long, pliable branches of certain shrubs can be bent to the ground and pegged into a position so that there is soil contact. A root system will be established where the branch remains in contact with the soil. Rhododendron, forsythia, and viburnum are particularly easy to grow this way. At the point where the branch touches the ground, it is best to scratch away the bark on the underside. This hastens the rooting process. Soil contact can be maintained by pegging the branch in position with a bent wire. A light covering of leaf mold or sphagnum moss will help prevent the layered part from drying out. If the soil is kept moist, within a year the plant will usually be sufficiently well-rooted to be cut from its parent and transplanted to another area of the garden.

Air Layering In addition to soil layering, described above, certain shrubs such as Rhododendron (including azaleas), Mock-orange (*Philadelphus coronarius*), and Firethorn

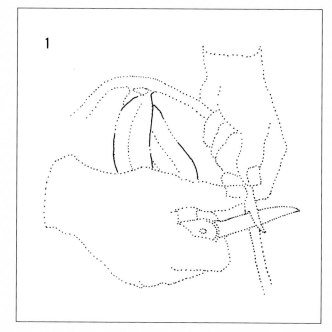

1

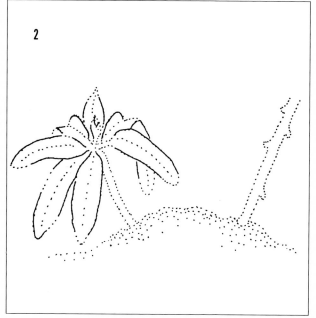

2

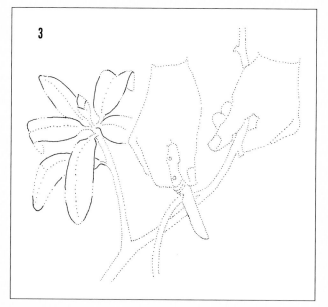

3

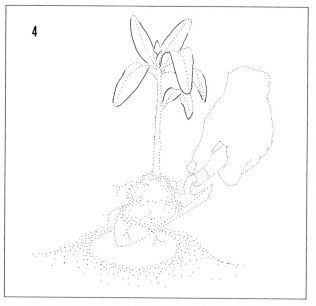

4

AIR LAYERING *(Opposite page)*

1-Scrape away the cambium.

2-Add spaghnum moss and cover with a plastic bag.

3-Cover the plastic with aluminum foil; use a twist tie to attach it to the shrub.

4-Cut off below the new roots and plant in the ground.

SOIL LAYERING *(Left)*

1-Branch to be layered should be slit to depth of bark where the branch touches the soil.

2-Pile soil over the cut and anchor with a piece of bent wire.

3-After layered branch is rooted (usually after several months), cut from parent.

4-Lift rooted end from soil with trowel for transplanting to a new location.

A FOOLPROOF WAY TO GROW SHRUBS FROM CUTTINGS —INDOORS

A common plastic freezer bag from your own kitchen can be turned into a mini-greenhouse for root cuttings.

The idea is to create a self-contained environment with its own humid micro-climate. Woody cuttings may take eight weeks to root. Cuttings which lose their leaves, turn brown, or wither should be removed or discarded.

1. Mix together equal parts of peat and sand, or peat and perlite, or peat and vermiculite. Alternatively, use a packaged propagating mix, ready-formulated from your local garden supply center. When using sand it should be salt-free, not the kind found at the beach.

2. Wet the mixture to make it evenly moist, just enough so that when you squeeze it tightly a few drops of water will appear.

(*Ptyracantha coccinea*) can be air layered. To do this, simply select a healthy portion of branch and scrape away about 1 inch of bark, completely encircling the branch. Then, take some moist sphagnum moss or a household sponge soaked with water, and cover the cut area. Hold it in place and secure a sheet of clear plastic around it with an elastic band or twist tie. Some air layers started in the spring will have formed a healthy root system by the end of the summer. Others, especially in colder climates, may take up to a year to produce visible roots. When roots are visible through the plastic, cut the rooted branch from the mother plant using a sharp knife or hand pruners, and plant in the garden.

GROWING SHRUBS IN CONTAINERS

Even though there are more colorful, longer-lasting plants to consider for decorating containers, many shrubs provide a sophisticated beauty in their shape and form (Japanese maples, for example), flowering longevity (roses, for example), and vertical accent (hollies and yews, for example). In fact, there has been such a great demand for shrubs and small trees that will grow in containers, that special hybrids have been developed for this purpose.

The bigger the container, the easier it will be to grow a shrub in it. Tubs of all kinds are fine, although a ten gallon minimum capacity is usually needed to accommodate enough soil for the large root system of most shrubs. The best containers to use are made of wood or clay, which help keep the soil cool on hot days when the root systems can be burned. Plastic and metal containers should not be used because they heat up rather than insulate the root system.

A very effective shrub container is called a "Versailles planter," so named because it is a popular feature in the Sunken Garden at the Palace of Versailles, located outside of Paris, France. It is a square, wooden planter, painted white or green, and supported on casters so it can be wheeled about. The beautiful and practical Versailles planter is especially good for growing tender shrubs, because it is easy to roll indoors during the cold winter months. For this reason peo-

ple choose to grow exotic shrubs in it, like dwarf orange trees, angel's trumpets, camellias, and gardenias, which merely require frost exclusion to keep them alive through the winter.

Generally, the commercial soil mixtures used with shrubs are too light on their own to anchor a shrub or small tree in a container. Therefore, it is a good practice to blend these potting mixes with sand to provide a greater density. Two ingredients commonly combined with potting soils are *vermiculite*, a lightweight, gritty rock, and *perlite*, a porous, volcanic rock. Besides helping to anchor the shrub in its pot, both have the ability to absorb water like a sponge and hold it for long periods of time, preventing rapid dehydration. They also add aeration for healthy development of roots.

3. Take a two quart plastic freezer bag and fill with about four inches of your propagating mixture. The bag must be free of holes so when it is sealed there will be no moisture loss.

4. Insert the cuttings so that they do not touch each other or the sides of the plastic bag.

5. Sprinkle the cuttings lightly with water—just enough to moisten the foliage. This is the last watering they will need until they are rooted.

6. Seal the top of the bag tightly with a rubber band. Place on a windowsill that receives no direct sunlight (north and west exposure). Leave the bag alone until the cuttings have had a chance to root.

Container shrubs need watering regularly, sometimes as much as once a day. You can test for moisture by plunging a finger about 2 inches into the pot. If the soil is dry, water it. Container shrubs can be watered with a garden hose, a watering can, or by installing a drip line connected to an irrigation system. Some irrigation systems have sets of long tubes with a nozzle on the end that drips moisture to feed numerous container plants at the turn of a faucet.

Container shrubs also need frequent fertilizing, approximately once every two weeks. Simply mix a liquid fertilizer with a gallon of water, and water as usual, or use a granular, timed-release fertilizer. A timed-release fertilizer releases its nutrients into the soil slowly (up to several months) and so saves you time.

PEST AND DISEASE CONTROL

In spite of their capacity to live long and healthy lives, shrubs are vulnerable to attack from various pests and diseases. Among the pests that can inflict severe damage are borers, scale insects, spider mites, and whiteflies. The best prevention against problems from insects, pests, and diseases, is healthy plants, kept in good condition by timely watering during dry spells and fertilizing each year.

Pests

Scale Insects commonly infect camellias, aucuba, and Japanese aralia. The most telling symptom is bulbs attached to the succulent part of the stems. These bulbs can be white, brown, gray, red, or yellow in color. If these areas are scaped with a fingernail, the soft underside of the insect will be revealed. Because scale insects suck the juices out of plants, once infected, the leaves generally turn yellow and the branches start to die. One treatment method requires spraying with an insecticide specifically marked "For treatment of scale." An alternative is to dip a cotton swab in rubbing alcohol and swabbing the pests off of the plant. This must be done every week, as eggs are newly hatching.

Borers, usually the burrowing caterpillars of night-flying moths, commonly infect rhododendrons, ornamental

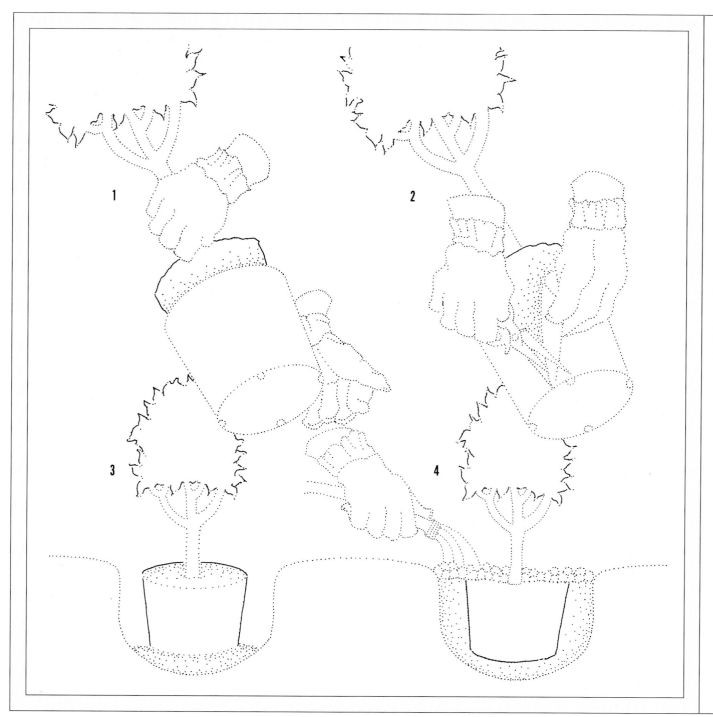

PLANTING SHRUBS FROM CONTAINERS

1. Gently tug the root ball to see if it will slide out of the container easily. Run a knife blade around the edge of the container if necessary.

2. If root ball resists, cut the container with a pair of heavy-duty scissors.

3. Place the root ball on a mound of topsoil.

4. Fill the hole to 1 inch of the soil line. Water. Tamp soil down. Supply wood chip mulch to deter weeds and conserve moisture.

Opposite page: A fruiting lemon tree in a terra cotta tub has its trunk ringed with daisies for added ornamental effect.

Right: A beautiful shrub border featuring azaleas and rhododendrons decorates a woodland walk.

Opposite page: Here, a wisteria vine is trained to a single trunk and pruned to three layers of branches to create a tree form. Each layer is held horizontally by an "umbrella" of metal spokes.

almonds, dogwoods, and lilacs. Some infected plants exude a gummy sap where the borer entered, but in many plants it's difficult to detect penetration by borers. Other signs include a branch that suddenly wilts, and bark that flakes away easily, revealing tunnels and holes where the borers are at work. Once these pests have entered a shrub they are extremely difficult to control, especially if they have entered the main trunk or the main multiple trunks. If only one branch seems to be infected, prune it away immediately. There is a compound you can buy in a tube, called Borekil, that you squeeze into the hole, gassing the borers; however, this kind of treatment is usually only good when there are just one or two borers to kill. The best remedy is to spray the base of shrubs with Lindane insecticide which kills the larvae as they hatch, and before they have a chance to enter the plant.

Spider mites are troublesome for rhododendrons, azaleas, camellias, and many other shrubs with fleshy leaves. They colonize plants and debilitate them by draining their juices. Signs of infestation include: yellowing leaves that take on a dusty, dirty appearance and curl at the ends, and a fine webbing on the undersides. If you hold a piece of white paper under a leaf and tap it sharply, tiny red, yellow, and lime green specks will drop down and crawl about.

To be effective, controls must be administered early in the infestation stage. Spray with Kelthane, making sure the pesticide reaches the underside of the leaves and branches. Repeat as needed. Spraying mite populations with a strong jet of water from a garden hose, if done on a regular basis, is also helpful in dislodging webs and colonies.

Whiteflies are small, white winged insects that colonize the underside of leaves. They are a problem mostly for shrubs grown under glass, especially camellias and gardenias. When a branch is shaken they rise in a cloud of white and flutter about. An indication that your shrubs are infested are sickly looking leaves that turn yellow and drop; the leaves may also have a black, sooty mold on them. You will also notice a sticky excrement coating the stems and leaves. If your shrubs do become infected with whiteflies, spray with an insecticide such as Diazinon.

In general, a good way to help combat a recurring pest problem with plants in containers is to repot the plant, as eggs can sometimes remain in the soil.

Diseases

By far the most serious shrub diseases are caused by fungi either entering the foliage canopy or attacking the roots. Though different strains of fungi attack different areas, the following are generally widespread:

Flower blight is especially troublesome on camellias and azaleas, with different strains affecting each type of plant. However, the symptoms for all strains are similar: The petals will start to turn brown until the entire flower drops off.

To prevent flower blight, spray flowers with Benomyl as soon as they reach the mature bud stage. Spray the ground before flowering begins, and clean up all infected debris. Destroy by burning. This fungus is especially prevalent in the Southern states and other humid climate areas.

Dieback is a fungus that enters the plant through wounds in branches. Usually the lower regions of the plant may look infected first. The leaves will turn brown but remain attached to the plant. Unfortunately, once a plant is infected, cure is impossible, except to prune away and burn the affected areas. The following season, spray with a copper based fungicide after blooming.

Powdery mildew shows itself as gray, powdery patches on leaves. This fungus is troublesome to lilacs, euonymus, and hydrangeas. Though the disease rarely kills a plant, it hampers photosynthesis, thus weakening them. The disease is most prevalent in the summer, during wet weather. It can be combatted by spraying with Benomyl.

Other physiological disorders not caused by pests or diseases, but conditions in the environment, can affect shrubs. These include:

Chlorosis, a yellowing of leaves caused by a deficiency of iron. The leaf veins of a plant with chlorosis will become prominent. To cure, increase soil acidity for such acid-loving plants as azaleas, pieris, and rhododendrons. This is done by adding peat moss or a similar organic content to the soil, or by adding aluminum sulphate according to the label directions. For non-acid-loving plants, increase overall fertility with a general-purpose fertilizer.

Salt burn is evident by the browning of the tips of leaves, especially in older plants. This occurs because salt builds up in soil from over-fertilizing, and the rainfall has not been sufficient to flush away this build up. It may also occur as a result of salt being used on the road or on walkways. Salt burn most often occurs with plants in containers, which are constantly being fed fertilizers. To cure, flush the soil thoroughly.

Windburn can be distinguished from salt burn since it is usually the younger leaves on the plant that suffer first, turning brown and brittle. The side facing prevailing winds will usually show the first symptoms. Windburn takes its heaviest toll in winter, when cold, searing winds chill and dehydrate the plant. To cure, some form of shelter is needed on the side facing prevailing winds. In extremely exposed locations the entire plant may need to be encircled with burlap. A dry Indian summer—where a lack of rainfall occurs prior to cold winter temperatures—makes shrubs particularly susceptible for they may enter winter dormancy lacking moisture. To counteract this, water in fall and even during the winter to replenish much-needed soil moisture.

TEN QUESTIONS FREQUENTLY ASKED ABOUT SHRUBS

1. *Why doesn't my flowering shrub bloom?* There are many reasons why a flowering shrub may not bloom. A few of the most common follow.

Do not expect flowers too soon after planting, as many shrubs suffer transplant shock and need two years to adjust to their new environment. Another common reason shrubs don't bloom is insufficient sunlight. Is the shrub in a deeply shaded area? Is heavy shade from an adjacent tree falling on it during the day? Perhaps the shrub needs feeding to replenish the nutrients in the soil. When a shrub starts to starve, the first part to suffer is often flower-bud formation.

Quite often, inappropriate pruning may be the culprit of a non-flowering, flowering shrub. For example, azaleas set new flower buds soon after flowering, but if the plant is sheared in late summer or early autumn, it will not have enough time before winter dormancy to initiate more flower buds. Also, winterkill of flowering buds can be a problem. Another problem may be that during an early spring thaw, the buds can

begin to swell; but, if a heavy freeze sets in, this can kill the immature flower parts inside the bud. This frequently happens to azaleas, rhododendrons, and forsythia in colder climates.

2. *What flowering shrubs can I plant in shade?* By far the best choice would be azaleas, though they like a lot of air circulation, so the shading elements, such as a tree canopy, should be fairly high up. Camellias, rhododendrons, and hydrangeas are also good for shade.

3. *Which shrubs will flower all summer?* Not many, and those that do generally have small flowers. *Abelia* x *grandiflora* ('Glossy Abelia') is one, as is *Potentilla fruticosa* ('Bush Cinquefoil'). The polyantha rose, 'The Fairy,' and the new 'Meidiland' roses will bloom continuously through the summer. Many roses also have a propensity to "repeat bloom," flowering first in early summer when the nights are cool and then again in autumn when cool conditions return.

4. *Are there any good flowering ground covers?* There are some good low-spreading varieties of azaleas suitable for ground cover, including the North Tisbury hybrids. The blue-flowering periwinkle, *Vinca minor,* makes a good, durable, ground cover in sun or shade, producing blue, starlike flowers even before the last snows of winter, and continuing to flower for a month or more.

5. *Are there any easy-care flowering shrubs that don't need pruning?* Many shrubby vines can be left to their own devices, providing they have sufficient room to ramble. The following vines and shrubs require little pruning: *Campsis radicans* ('Trumpetvine'); weeping shrubs, such as *Forsythia spectabilis* ('Forsythia'); and *Prunus subhirtella* 'Pendula' ('Weeping Cherry'). Also, many kinds of slow-growing rhododendrons and azaleas require little or no pruning if they have sufficient room to grow.

6. *When a shrub looks sick, how can I get the problem diagnosed?* Call your local county extension agent and ask for instructions on where to send a specimen of the sickly looking parts; this will usually be a pest identification center, often located at your state land-grant university. You will quickly receive a diagnosis and recommended cure.

7. *What's the best way to fertilize shrubs?* Select a high-nitrogen fertilizer in granular form, and simply sprinkle it over the soil surface, raking it into the topsoil, without disturbing the roots. Rainfall or watering will then carry the nutrients to the feeder roots, mostly located near the soil surface. Extend the fertilizer application to slightly beyond the drip line. Mulching plants each year with organic material such as well-decomposed leaf mold, made from shredded leaves left in a pile for a year to break down, helps to replenish exhausted soil with nutrients. It is rich in plant nutrients and trace elements.

8. *What are some good shrubs for winter color?* Many shrubs that flower in spring or summer produce wonderful berry displays in autumn that often persist well into winter. The best berry-bearing shrubs are *Ilex verticillata* ('Winterberry'), *Pyracantha coccinea* ('Scarlet Firethorn'), *Berberis koreana* (Korean Barberry), and *Ilex* x *meservae* ('Blue Holly'). For flowering effect, plant *Hamamelis mollis* ('Witch-hazel'), which blooms in late winter and early spring at the first sign of a warming trend, even before early spring-flowering bulbs.

9. *What are other good flowering shrubs, like rhododendrons, that bloom later in the year?* *Rosea* species ('Roses'), *Lagerstroemia indica* ('Crepe-myrtle'), *Hydrangea* ('Hydrangea'), and berry-bearing viburnums, like *Viburnum dilatatum.*

10. *What's the best flowering hedge?* Probably, types of polyantha roses, such as 'Robin Hood'; also azaleas. Firethorn (*Pyracantha coccinea*) makes a great decorative hedge because of its beautiful berries, and the leaves of burning bush (*Euonymus alata*) have a brilliant red autumn color as intense as any red azalea, even though its flowers are inconspicuous.

Opposite page: Trees and shrubs planted along a grassy walk create a beautiful vista leading from the house to the bottom of the property. Dogwoods extend color high into the sky.

Left: The maze at Deerfield Garden, Rydal, Pennsylvania, is a half-size replica of the maze at Hampton Court, in England. Planted from English boxwood, the maze is kept at 4 feet high by pruning only once a year, since the natural growth rate of boxwood is just 1 inch a year.

Right: A vista with parallel shrub borders edging a grass path. Flowering dogwoods illuminate the canopy.

CHAPTER TWO

DESIGNING WITH SHRUBS

I**T IS NOT AS EASY FOR SHRUBS TO MAKE AN** impact in the landscape as it is for more colorful and faster-flowering annuals, perennials, and bulbs. Instead of providing color, shrubs are used more for their structural beauty; they add height and form to garden design concepts, and highlight the area beneath a canopy of trees. Certain shrubs are used for purely functional reasons: they have a desirable quality, such as dense habit, that makes them suitable as permanent plantings. Some of these functions are as sentinals to an entranceway, as hedges delineating corridors and the movement of traffic, and as barriers. No one could argue that in flower or fruit many shrubs match the dramatic color impact of the showiest annuals. What could be more stunning than a bougainvillea vine, a kurume azalea, or a floribunda rose in flower? The many shrub designs are described below.

Mixed Shrub Borders consist of a collection of plants arranged according to the effect produced by their color, texture, and form. Mixing needle evergreens and broadleaf evergreens with deciduous shrubs of all shapes and sizes produces a pleasant visual effect. Usually, any flowering types of shrubs are chosen to produce a color impact at a particular time of year—usually spring—so that something is always coming into bloom, except during the winter months. Care must be taken to plant shrubs with the right spacing so

that as they grow and mature they can attain their maximum height and width—kept within bounds, of course, by timely pruning. In mixed shrub borders, plants are chosen for three distinct heights: low growing, medium height, and tall. Some plants should be left to grow informally to produce an irregular outline, while others should be pruned to create cushions, which have a soothing effect. Others may be pruned into such shapes as cones and spires to achieve height and accentuate the architectural lines of a nearby wall or building. Mixed shrub borders tend to be situated away from the house so they can be admired from a window.

Top: Evergreen yews and flowering azaleas combine with creeping phlox to make a colorful foundation planting.

Bottom: Flowering dogwood underplanted with azaleas brighten up an entrance to a suburban home.

Foundation plantings are generally collections of shrubs situated along the foundation of a house. Their purpose is to soften the stark lines of a wall, to disguise monotonous expanses of concrete and brick, and to make the house look attractive from the road or other vantage points. Many foundation plantings are composed entirely of evergreens to make them easy to care for. Their appearance is enhanced by timely pruning, allowing the creation of mounds, spires, cones, and other rounded, vertical, or horizontal shapes. More imaginative foundation plantings include flowering plants, especially azaleas, camellias, and hydrangeas, with enough space left between for a splash of seasonal color from clumps of annuals, perennials, and flowering bulbs.

Foundation plants should be planted so that they complement the lines of the house and will not obscure any windows. For example, at a corner, a vertical highlight, such as a tall juniper, can accentuate the perpendicular line more successfully than a low, spreading shrub like an azalea, which is better suited to be planted under a window.

In new houses, debris may have been left by the builders; therefore, it is important to excavate beds to a good soil depth (at least 2 feet) and add quality soil with plenty of humus. Similarly, consideration should be given to exposure: is the foundation planting on a sunny side of the house or a shaded side of the house? This will help determine what types of shrubs to plant.

When planning and preparing your foundation site, you must also take into account what type of mulch to use. Be careful about using limestone landscape chips as a mulch around acid-loving plants like hollies, azaleas, and rhododendrons. The pH of the soil can be affected to such an extent that these plants will struggle to survive unless an adjustment is made with a soil amendment such as Miracid.

Rock Gardens Many kinds of evergreen shrubs look especially attractive planted in a rock garden, as they serve to break up what might otherwise be a rather bleak or barren landscape. Tall, spirelike junipers can be planted to provide vertical accents, while low-spreading cotoneasters and hypericum can carpet the ground and cascade over rocks. Mounded shrubs like mugo pines can decorate the landscape like cushions, while billowing forms like rhododendrons can create a beautiful, dark green background or

Left: A rich assortment of shrubs, specially chosen to present a pleasing arrangement of shapes and textures, decorate a rocky slope at Bishop's Close, a garden overlooking the Willamette River, Portland, Oregon.

Opposite page: A billowing hedge of English boxwood creates an intimate sitting area between a flower-bordered lawn and the wall of a house.

Right: It is possible to be quite creative when designing the shrubs. Some unusual forms are seen at right.

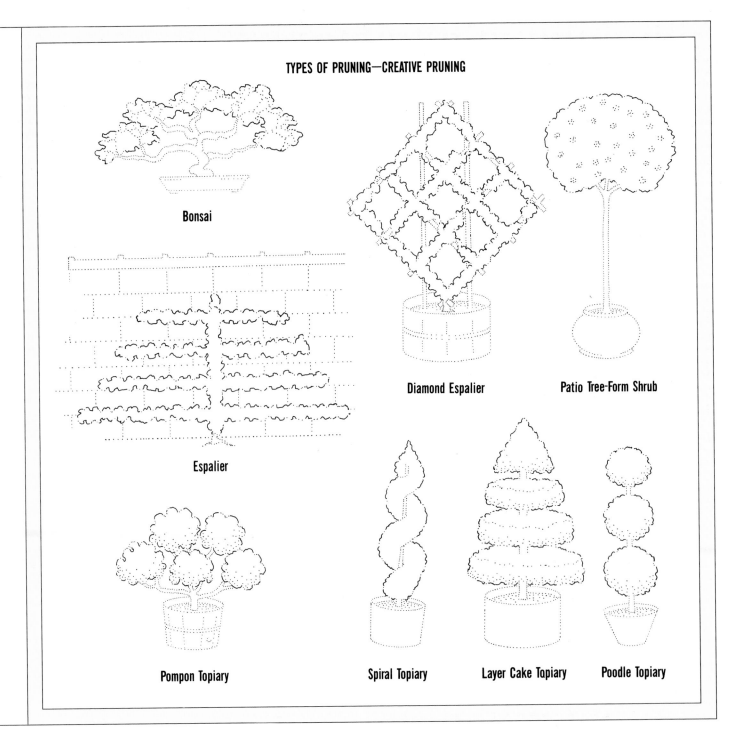

TYPES OF PRUNING—CREATIVE PRUNING

Bonsai

Diamond Espalier

Patio Tree-Form Shrub

Espalier

Pompon Topiary

Spiral Topiary

Layer Cake Topiary

Poodle Topiary

windbreak against which the rock garden can be admired. Usually, rock gardens are situated on slopes with a sunny exposure, so the soil is likely to be on the dry side, thus demanding plants that tolerate drought. Solutions to this dry soil problem may be to thread the rock garden with streams and waterfalls or irrigate with drip lines, allowing moisture-loving plants to be added to the landscape.

Parterres are low hedges that outline planting beds. Sometimes they are simple, geometric shapes like diamonds and squares; other times they are extremely elaborate swirls, scrolls, and flourishes. Usually a parterre is situated near a tall structure, such as a tower or tall building, so that the decorative outlines can be seen to their best advantage. Effective parterres generally need dwarf shrubs with dense, evergreen growth, like boxwood.

Hedges can be planted in a straight line to make a barrier, or in parallel lines to form corridors directing movement from one area of the garden to another. Hedges can also serve as windbreaks, cushioning the force of winds, and as screens to provide privacy. Tall hedges can be pruned to make windows and archways. Effective hedges need to be fairly fast-growing and capable of forming a dense mass of intermingling branches and branchlets that knit together to make an impenetrable barrier. Though evergreens are generally the preferred choice for hedges, many deciduous shrubs that drop their leaves in autumn can still present an impenetrable living wall from their tightly interwoven twigs; some even have the added distinction of thorns to resist penetration.

Since the idea of a hedge is for each plant to merge into its neighbor, negating any apparent distinction from one plant to another, shrubs grown for this purpose are generally planted closer together than normal. Generally, hedges in small gardens are sheared to maintain straight sides, while hedges that form boundaries of properties are left to grow untamed.

Mazes are hedges planted in parallel lines, either straight or curved, to form a labyrinth. The first hedge maze in the world, constructed at Hampton Court Palace, England, in the 1700s, still exists today. A copy of this famous Tudor-design maze can be seen on the grounds of the Governor's Palace, at Colonial Williamsburg, in Virginia, and at Deerfield Garden, near Philadelphia, Pennsylvania. Usually, a mound is located near the maze so that the people standing

Right: An English yew splayed out like a fan softens the lines of a stone wall.

Below: Firethorn makes an especially good subject for espalier plantings because of the colorful berries that persist well into winter.

Opposite page: Wisteria vine, trained along metal supports, forms a flowering arbor beside the pond in Claude Monet's garden in Giverny, France. The painter planted this wisteria almost 100 years ago.

on top of the mound can see over the hedges and direct those in the maze to the center and out again. Good hedge material for mazes includes holly, hemlock, and Japanese yew, though the very best is generally English boxwood. Unfortunately, English boxwood grows extremely slowly, but when pruned its lines are clean and sharp.

Whether planting a parterre, hedge, or maze, it is extremely important to provide good soil. In the absence of good soil, dig a trench 1 to 2 feet deep and fill it with humus-rich topsoil trucked to the site or taken from another area of your garden. You want every plant to be given an equal chance of survival and to last a long time, so it's worth the extra effort of ensuring good soil. To create your parterre, hedge, or maze layout, use string tied to stakes for a straight design, and a garden hose for a curved design.

Topiary was first used by the Romans, and later popularized by the British. It is the pruning of shrubs into whimsical shapes and figures. Suitable specimens to use for topiary include Japanese yew, hemlock, English boxwood, and holly.

Usually, the shrub is grown in soil and its growth habit is kept compact by continued shearing until it is large enough to trim with pruning shears. Some popular topiary designs are swans, crowns, chess pieces, and even giraffes. A faster way of creating a topiary accent is to make a wire form and fill it with moist sphagnum moss. Then a creeping vine like English ivy is planted to hug the frame and fill out the shape. These "quick" topiaries can be started in pots and moved about from place to place, even indoors.

Espalier is a method of training shrubs or small trees so they make a flat pattern against a wall or fence. Common shrubs to use include dwarf pears, dwarf apples, firethorn, and yew. Care must be taken to ensure that the wall is not too light-reflective. Stucco walls, for example, can be extremely harsh for espaliered fruit trees, burning the embryo fruits so they never mature, and scorching the wood. For fruit trees a brick wall or wooden fence is preferable. Some shrubs, such as apples and pears, have such pliable limbs, they can be trained along wires or wooden rails to form "ropes" (botanically called cordons). The added air circulation of this form of espalier generally encourages fruit. These cordons are especially good for making a low edging or fence to define an herb garden, vegetable garden, or border.

SMALL CIRCULAR BED

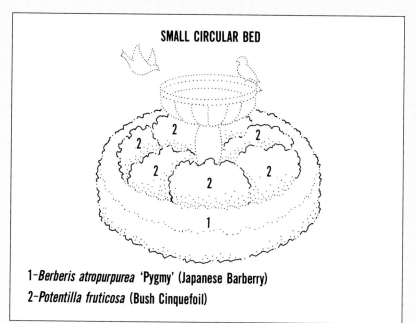

1-*Berberis atropurpurea* 'Pygmy' (Japanese Barberry)

2-*Potentilla fruticosa* (Bush Cinquefoil)

CONTAINER PLANTS FOR A DECK

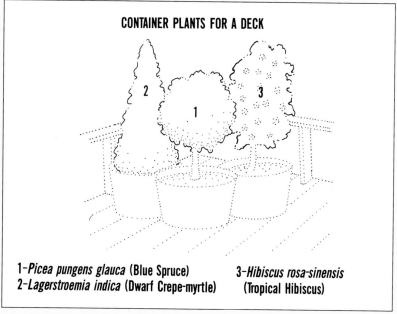

1-*Picea pungens glauca* (Blue Spruce)
2-*Lagerstroemia indica* (Dwarf Crepe-myrtle)

3-*Hibiscus rosa-sinensis*
(Tropical Hibiscus)

DOORWAY PLANTING

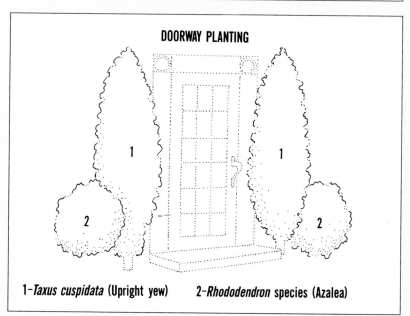

1-*Taxus cuspidata* (Upright yew)   2-*Rhododendron* species (Azalea)

BORDER PLANTING ALONG A FENCE

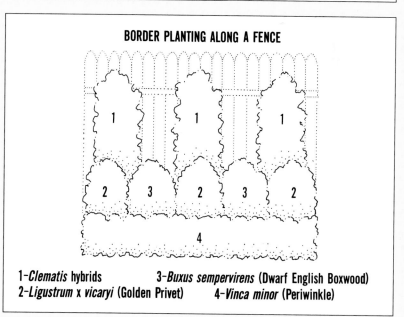

1-*Clematis* hybrids   3-*Buxus sempervirens* (Dwarf English Boxwood)
2-*Ligustrum x vicaryi* (Golden Privet)   4-*Vinca minor* (Periwinkle)

Right: **An Atlas cedar makes a beautiful bonsai specimen, with copper wire used to hold branches in place.**

Far right: **A pair of forsythia, planted on either side of a gate, make colorful sentinels in early spring.**

Opposite page: **A collection of azaleas, pruned to mounded shapes, creates a colorful shrub border.**

Avenues are the perfect complement for driveways. Plant the edges of the driveway with cone-shaped shrubs to make a formal entryway or with billowing shrubs, such as forsythia, spiraea, hydrangea, and azalea to create a sweep of color.

Archways are best for side entrances and pathways leading through gardens, as they can completely cover the walk with a canopy of leafy and flowering vines. Good shrubs to work with include wisteria, honeysuckle, trumpet creepers, and climbing roses.

Sentinels are pairs of attractive shrubs that stand on either side of a gate or doorway. They can be planted in soil or grown in containers (see "Growing Shrubs In Containers", page 29). Some good shrubs to consider as sentinels include upright yews, podocarpus, upright junipers, star magnolias, quince, hemlock, and firethorn espaliered against a wall.

Ground cover Many creeping or low-spreading shrubs can be planted in a mass knit together to form a luxurious, dense mass of leaves through which weeds cannot grow. The very best, durable ground covers for sun include Blue Rug juniper, hypericum, cotoneaster, and red barberry. For shade, consider vinca, English ivy, pachysandra, and dwarf azalea. Consider tough, durable candidates for erosion control on slopes. Low-spreading forms of forsythia, banksia roses, bearberry, azaleas, and ceanothus can be both functional and highly ornamental.

Windbreaks The problem with planting any shrub to create a windbreak is how to get it established. The solution is to build a temporary shelter from bales of hay or burlap sacking stapled to posts, sheltering the windbreak shrubs from prevailing winds until the plants themselves are sufficiently well-established to resist the wind on their own. Where winds are a constant problem, a double windbreak (consisting of two parallel rows of shrubs) may be necessary to completely dissipate the force of the wind. Usually, evergreens are preferred for windbreaks. Good windbreak shrubs include holly, pittosporum, rugosa rose, podocarpus, pines, junipers, and beach plum.

Bonsai is a skill requiring great patience, since it involves growing shrubs and trees in special shallow dishes. Confining the roots in this manner tends to restrict the height of the plant; by careful pruning, an illusion of great age or maturity can be created. Limbs can be bent into special contours and fixed in place by wires so that the shrubs take on the appearance of plants that have been weathered by exposure to winds on a mountaintop or salty air by the ocean. Special instruction by bonsai masters is needed to become adept at this fascinating art form. Some good shrubs that make terrific bonsai subjects include azaleas, camellias, calamondin orange, pomegranate, and plums. Though the plants can be kept miniature in the bonsai trays, the flowers and fruit that form are normal in size. Many evergreens are also favored as bonsai subjects, including pine, spruce, and juniper, sometimes planted as a miniature grove to create an illusionary bonsai forest.

WAYS TO USE SHRUBS IN THE LANDSCAPE

Left: Grow shrubs as a hedge along a fence or up a wall. Use shrubs as an island bed surrounded by paving. Grow shrubs in containers.

For an Arbor, use flowering vines such as *Campsis radicans* (Trumpetcreeper), *Wisteria sinensis* (Wisteria), climbing roses, and *Clematis jackmanii*.

For a Hedge, use flowering shrubs, especially *Abelia* x *grandiflora* (Glossy Abelia), *Azalea* hybrids, and *Hibiscus* species.

For Ground Cover Where Grass Will Not Grow, use shade-loving shrubs, such as *Vinca minor* (Periwinkle).

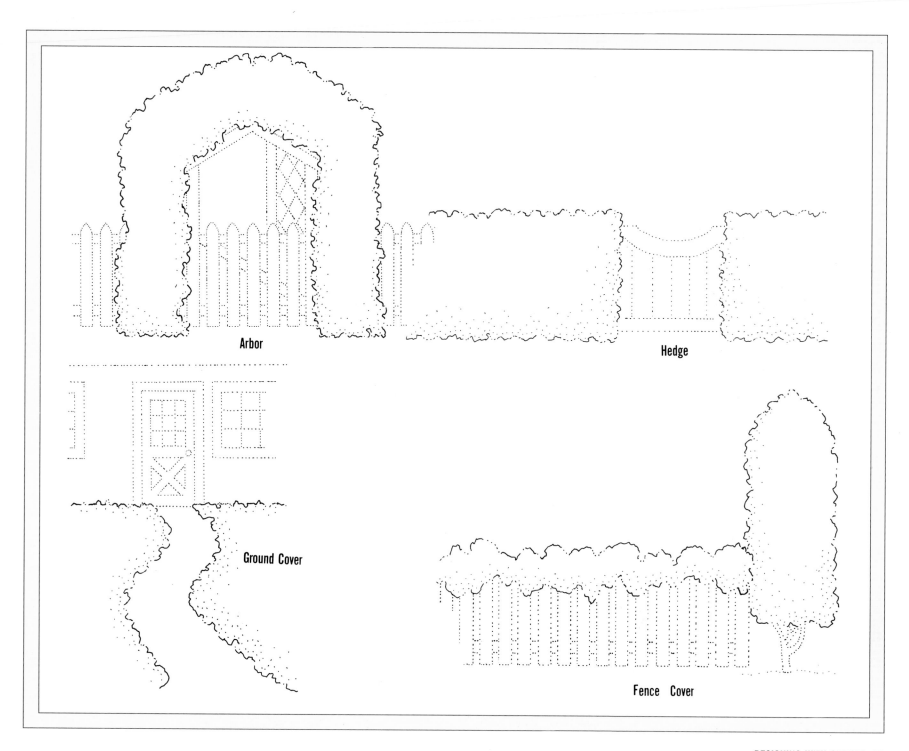

Arbor

Hedge

Ground Cover

Fence Cover

CHAPTER THREE

THE ENCYCLOPEDIA OF ESSENTIAL SHRUBS

T HE FOLLOWING SECTION DESCRIBES 100 deciduous and evergreen shrubs most often used in home landscaping. They include true shrubs, some small trees, a number of vines, and several good ground covers. Most are hardy, though a few exotic, tender varieties have been included for those gardeners fortunate enough to live in areas with mild winters. Some of the shrubs featured are noted for their flowering effect; others for functional reasons such as screening for privacy, hedges, topiary, and covering arbors.

Each shrub is listed first with its botanical (Latin) name, since this more accurately identifies the shrub than does its common name. While many shrubs have popular common names—'Holly' for *Ilex* species—others do not, or else they are known by two or more common names; *Caryopteris* x *clandonensis*, for example, is often called 'Blue Mist Shrub' or 'Bluebeard'.

To find a description for a shrub where you know only the common name, simply refer to the index for a quick cross reference.

The heights given are approximate. Often, with age and in good soil, plants may exceed the heights stated here. Also, the description for habit is the natural habit of the plant left to its own devices. Many shrubs described as 'billowing' or 'mounded' can be pruned into any desirable shape.

BOTANICAL NAME *Abelia* x *grandiflora*

COMMON NAME Glossy Abelia

RANGE Tolerates zone 5 but prefers zone 6 and further south. Stem kill occurs at -5° to -10°F.

HEIGHT 3 to 5 feet tall and equally as wide; medium-sized shrub.

CULTURE Moist, well-drained, acidic soil, in full to partial sun. Propagated by cuttings.

DESCRIPTION Semi-evergreen. Grown primarily for its excellent, lustrous, dark green foliage that is paler green beneath. Leaves are 1 to 1½ inches long and take on a bronze color in the winter months. Flowers bloom from July until frost and are funnel-shaped, 3/4 of an inch long with white to pinkish blossoms. Fairly disease-resistant. Dislikes harsh, strong winds.

LANDSCAPE USE This spreading, dense, multi-stemmed shrub has arching branches that make a good hedge or bank cover. Prune to the height you want. Also used as a background or specimen plant. Plus, it combines well with broadleaf evergreens.

BOTANICAL NAME *Acer palmatum dissectum*

COMMON NAME Japanese Maple

RANGE Zones 5–8. Native to Japan and Korea.

HEIGHT Slow-growing, 15 to 20 feet tall, with a spread equal to or greater than height; mounded form, weeping branches.

CULTURE Thrives in moist, well-drained, and acidic soil in full sun or partial shade if the weather is hot and dry, with constant winds. Propagated by seed and cuttings.

DESCRIPTION Deciduous tree. Provides all-year interest: red growth in the spring, soft green lacey leaves in the summer, scarlet foliage in the fall, and a delicate, leafless silhouette during the winter. Flowers are small and purple, borne in clusters May through June.

LANDSCAPE USE One of the most flexible maple species for landscape uses. Attractive planted as a specimen tree for patios or entryways; in groves as woodland plants; as a background for ferns and azaleas; as an accent plant, shrub border, or bonsai planting. Since it naturally grows layers of leaves at the end of sinuous branches, pruning is rarely needed.

BOTANICAL NAME *Actinidia chinensis*

COMMON NAME Kiwi

RANGE Zone 7. Native to east Asia.

HEIGHT To 30 feet tall; twining vine, requires support.

CULTURE Prefers rich, sandy soil in full sun or partial shade. Rapid grower that needs regular pruning to hold shape or pattern. Propagated by seed.

DESCRIPTION Deciduous vine that is highly adaptable. Leaves are heart-shaped, lustrous, and dark green above with white, downy undersides. New growth looks like it is covered with a rich looking red fuzz. Flowers are 1 to 1½ inches wide with creamy white blooms that appear throughout May. Fruits are covered with brown fuzz and are somewhat egg-shaped. The lime-green flesh of the fruit is reminiscent of the taste of melon and banana. Both a male and a female plant are necessary for fruit set. A hardier species, *A. arguta* ('Bower Actinidia') has equally attractive leaves, and bears small, edible, green, grape-sized fruits.

LANDSCAPE USE Excellent quick vine cover that grows well in problem areas. Train to cover walls and fences or supply sturdy supports such as trellis, arbor, or patio, overhead.

BOTANICAL NAME *Allamanda cathartica* 'Williamsi'

COMMON NAME Yellow Allamanda; Henderson Common Allamanda

RANGE Zone 9. Native to Brazil.

HEIGHT Climbs to 10 feet or spreads as a shrub depending on pruning.

CULTURE Prefers rich soil in full sun. Feed regularly. Grows in only the warmest, most frost-free areas. Can be grown as a greenhouse plant. Propagated by cuttings.

DESCRIPTION Broadleaf evergreen. Dense foliage of thick, 6-inch long, roundish, dark green leaves. Yellow, saucer-shaped flowers, up to 4 inches across, bloom in June.

LANDSCAPE USE Evergreen vining shrub. Good to grow up a trellis or allow to cascade over low walls.

BOTANICAL NAME *Amelanchier arborea*

COMMON NAME Serviceberry

RANGE Zones 4–9. Native to North America.

HEIGHT Generally 15 to 25 feet tall with a variable spread, can grow as high as 40 feet; tree-like habit.

CULTURE Prefers well-drained, moist, acidic soil in full sun or partial shade. Commonly found in nature along woodland borders, streambanks, and fencerows in open meadows. Intolerant of pollution. Rarely needs pruning. Propagated by seed or division.

DESCRIPTION Deciduous shrub or small tree. Provides all season interest: showy clusters of white flowers appear in mid to late April; small, edible, purplish black round fruits ripen in June; medium to dark green leaves turn yellow, orange, and red in the fall; an attractive winter branch and twig pattern occurs in the winter. Rounded habit.

LANDSCAPE USE Widely used in landscaping. Stunning planted against a dark evergreen background to emphasize its delicate flowers and foliage. Excellent used for naturalistic plantings near the edges of woodlands, ponds, or streambanks. Berries attract birds.

BOTANICAL NAME *Ardisia japonica*

COMMON NAME Marlberry; Japanese Ardisia

RANGE Zones 8–9. Native to Japan and China.

HEIGHT 8 to 18 inches high; low-spreading shrub.

CULTURE Prefers an organic, moist, well-drained, acidic soil in partial or full shade. Propagated by division.

DESCRIPTION Broadleaf evergreen. Leathery, dark green leaves. White, star-shaped flowers bloom July through August, followed by brilliant scarlet fruits that last throughout the winter. Spreads rapidly.

LANDSCAPE USE Excellent shrub or ground cover to use in shady areas. Ideal choice for a woodland setting.

BOTANICAL NAME *Aucuba japonica* 'Variegata'

COMMON NAME Gold-dust Plant.

RANGE Zones 7–10, not reliably winter hardy in Zone 6. Native to Japan.

HEIGHT 5 to 10 feet tall; bushy habit.

CULTURE Prefers well-drained, moist, high organic soil in dappled shade. May need some winter protection. Can be grown as a houseplant. Propagated by root cuttings.

DESCRIPTION A tidy, broadleaf evergreen, upright, rounded shrub that is usually multi-stemmed. Dark, lustrous, showy leaves with yellow flecking. Small, purple flowers bloom March through April and are ornamentally unimportant. Red berries mature in October and November, and persist until spring.

LANDSCAPE USE An attractive understory plant. Good foundation planting on the north or east side of a home. If protected, it can make an effective evergreen border. Spruces up a dark corner and adds color to an all-green landscape.

BOTANICAL NAME *Beaumontia grandiflora*

COMMON NAME Herald's-trumpet; Easter Lily Vine

RANGE Zone 9; hardy to 28°F. Native to South America.

HEIGHT Up to 30 feet with equal spread; vine.

CULTURE Prefers deep, rich, moist soil in full sun. Heavy feeder. Prune back two and three-year old wood to preserve shape. Flowers are borne on old growth. Prune after flowering. Propagated by cuttings.

DESCRIPTION Broadleaf evergreen. Large lush, dark green, roundish leaves are shiny above with downy undersides. Fragrant, white, green-veined, 5-inch trumpet-shaped blooms resemble Easter lilies. Flowers bloom April through September.

LANDSCAPE USE Espalier on a wall sheltered from wind; train on a sturdy support or along the eaves of a house.

Right: A mixed shrub border at Andalusia Garden, near Philadelphia, Pennsylvania, features many evergreen shrubs accentuated against the flowering forms of dogwood and broom.

BOTANICAL NAME *Berberis thunbergii atropurpurea*

COMMON NAME Japanese Barberry

RANGE Zones 4–8. Native to Japan.

HEIGHT 4 to 6 feet tall with equal spread; bushy habit.

CULTURE Grows in a variety of soils and climates. Very hardy. Excellent for harsh climates. Shear to maintain a tidy shape. Prune to ground level in late winter to rejuvenate plants. Propagated by cuttings.

DESCRIPTION Compact, rounded, deciduous shrub that can look untidy if not pruned. Vigorous grower that requires full sun to develop leaf color. One of first shrubs to leaf out in spring. Green leaves turn a bronzy to purplish red in the summer. Inconspicuous, small yellow flowers bloom mid April through May. Attractive red fruit persists through winter and attracts birds.

LANDSCAPE USE Planted for its foliage color, fruit, and its rounded, multi-stemmed shape. Tolerates urban conditions quite well. Use as a hedge, barrier, and in groupings.

RELATED SPECIES *Berberis koreana*, ('Korean Barberry'), whose bright red berries persist into winter.

BOTANICAL NAME *Bougainvillea spectabilis*

COMMON NAME Bougainvillea; Brazil Bougainvillea

RANGE Zone 9–10. Hardy in tropical climates.

HEIGHT Grows to 20 feet high; shrubby vine.

CULTURE Prefers well-drained, good garden soil in full sun; light shade in hottest areas. Protect from wind. If planted in a container, use rich soil. Where frost is expected, grow the vine in the warmest spot in the garden or on a protected wall. Plant in early spring to give longest possible growing season before frost. **Caution:** Plants don't like to be moved or repotted as this disturbs their root system. Handle with extreme care by cutting open the pot or cutting out the bottom before placing plants in a larger container or in the ground. Prune to renew, shape, or direct growth of plants. Propagated by cuttings.

DESCRIPTION Showy, trailing shrub grown for its vibrant yellow to purplish magenta colors. The small white flowers are ornamentally unimportant and are almost hidden between the showy, colorful bracts. Leaves are medium green or variegated on thorny stems.

LANDSCAPE USE Heavily pruned plants can be used as container shrubs for patio or terrace. Otherwise, use as a sprawling vine on a sturdy structure or as a sprawling shrub for banks and ground covers. Grow under glass where freezing winters occur.

BOTANICAL NAME *Brunfelsia calycina floribunda*

COMMON NAME Yesterday, Today, Tomorrow

RANGE Zone 9. Native to Brazil.

HEIGHT About 10 feet, but may be held to 3 feet by pruning; bushy habit.

CULTURE Rich, well-drained, moist, acidic soil in partial shade. Heavy feeder during growing season. Prune in spring to hold shape and to remove untidy growth. Propagated by cuttings.

DESCRIPTION Named after the quick color change of its blossoms: purple ("yesterday"), lavender ("today"), and white ("tomorrow"). Tubular-shaped flowers, borne in clusters, bloom profusely in the spring. Broadleaf evergreen shrub that loses most of its foliage for a short period of time in non-tropical climates. Leaves are about 4 inches long, dark green above, pale green below.

LANDSCAPE USE Good for use in containers or as a showy specimen plant. Grow under glass where freezing winters occur.

BOTANICAL NAME *Buddleia davidii*

COMMON NAME Butterfly Bush

RANGE Zones 5–9. In cold climates the soft wood freezes to the ground but roots remain hardy. Native to China.

HEIGHT 3 to 10 feet high; bushy habit.

CULTURE Prefers well-drained, fertile soil in full sun. Propagated by cuttings.

DESCRIPTION Deciduous shrub. Vigorous grower that is almost weedlike. Lance-shaped leaves are dark green above, downy white below. In mid-summer, dense, arching, spikelike clusters appear with small, fragrant lilac flowers with orange eyes. Attracts butterflies.

LANDSCAPE USE Good summer-flowering specimen plant. Attractive in shrub or perennial borders. Suitable for containers.

BOTANICAL NAME *Buxus sempervirens*

COMMON NAME English Boxwood

RANGE Zones 5–9. Native of southern Europe, northern Africa, and western Asia.

HEIGHT Generally 15 to 20 feet tall with equal spread but can grow to 30 feet; bushy habit.

CULTURE Adaptable but prefers warm, moist climates. Likes moist, well-drained, high organic soil. Tolerates full sun to partial shade. Keep roots cool. Some winter protection is often necessary. Keep the evergreen leaves cleared of ice and snow to prevent "browning". Prune by shearing to maintain shape. Propagated by cuttings.

DESCRIPTION Slow-growing broadleaf evergreen shrub. Easy to maintain. Grown for its dense foliage of medium-sized, lustrous, dark green, oval leaves. Flowers and fruit are ornamentally unimportant.

LANDSCAPE USE An excellent plant for foundations, formal gardens, hedges, and edging.

BOTANICAL NAME *Calliandra haematocephala*

COMMON NAME Powderpuff Shrub

RANGE Zones 9–10. Native to Bolivia.

HEIGHT 16 feet high, 10 feet wide; mounded, bushy habit.

CULTURE Moist, well-drained, average soil in full sun. Propagated by seed.

DESCRIPTION Evergreen. Grown for its brillant, scarlet, large powderpuff of silky flowers that bloom October through March. The fruit consists of a flat pod with thickened margins. Dark green, velvety, rich leaves.

LANDSCAPE USE Popular accent shrub in California, southern Florida, and Hawaii. Prefers a warm, sunny site and makes an ideal plant for espalier.

BOTANICAL NAME *Callicarpa japonica*

COMMON NAME Japanese Beauty Berry

RANGE Zones 5-8. Native to Japan.

HEIGHT 6 to 10 feet tall, but is usually pruned to hold shape at 3 feet; bushy, arching habit.

CULTURE Grows in any well-drained soil in full sun. Tolerates light shade. Propagated by cuttings or ground layering.

DESCRIPTION Deciduous shrub. Grown primarily for its colorful, purple berries that are borne in clusters along arching stems in the fall. Berries last two to three weeks after the leaves fall. Small white or pink flowers bloom in midsummer and are hidden beneath 2- to 4-inch green leaves. Leaves turn a golden color in autumn. Plant is often pruned in the spring to 4 to 6 inches from the ground in order to produce a bountiful crop of berries. In colder climates, plant freezes to the ground and reappears in the spring as a young shoot.

LANDSCAPE USE Effective planted in groups in a shrub border. Berries attract birds.

BOTANICAL NAME *Callistemon citrinus*

COMMON NAME Lemon Bottlebrush

RANGE Zones 9–10. Native to Australia.

HEIGHT Grows to 10 to 15 feet tall. With pruning and staking, can be trained to a narrow, roundish tree, 20 to 25 feet tall. Massive shrub.

CULTURE Prefers moist, well-drained, sandy soil in full sun. Tolerates drought, wind, neglect, salt air, and alkaline soil. Propagated by seed.

DESCRIPTION Broadleaf evergreen. Vivid green leaves are 3 inches long, willow-like. Leaves are lightly fragrant, emitting a faint lemon scent when bruised. Pendant, 6-inch crimson flower clusters are showy with conspicuous yellow stamens. A hard, rounded fruit surrounds the flowering stems.

LANDSCAPE USE This spreading shrub can be trained as a street or garden tree. Good used as a windbreak hedge, screen, or espalier; versatile. Can be grown under glass in colder climates.

BOTANICAL NAME *Calluna vulgaris*

COMMON NAME Scotch Heather

RANGE Zones 4–7. Native to Europe, Asia Minor, and has naturalized in northeastern North America.

HEIGHT 15 to 30 inches tall; upright, bushy habit.

CULTURE Prefers sandy, organic, moist, well-drained, acidic soil that is not too fertile, in full sun or partial shade. Avoid sweeping winds as plants are susceptible to drying. Prune by shearing in early spring before new growth starts. Mulch to retain moisture. Propagated by seed or cuttings.

DESCRIPTION There are hundreds of cultivars. Upright, branching, small broadleaf evergreen. Dense leaves and stems form thick mounds. Leaf color may vary from a medium green to orange-red. The urn-shaped flowers bloom from July to September. Flower color includes white, rose, and purplish pink.

LANDSCAPE USE Attracts bees. Excellent ground cover. Good for edging and slope cover.

BOTANICAL NAME *Camellia japonica*

COMMON NAME Camellia

RANGE Zones 8–9. Native to the central coast of Japan, South Korea, and Taiwan.

HEIGHT 15 to 45 feet, spreading to 6 to 15 feet; generally kept to 6 to 12 feet by pruning; upright, bushy habit.

CULTURE Prefers well-drained, moist, acidic, humus-rich soil rich in organic material, in full sun. Prune after flowering to hold form. Shorten lower branches to encourage upright growth. Prune dead or weak growth to open up dense foliage and to enhance the showy blooms. Propagated by cuttings.

DESCRIPTION Broadleaf evergreen. Easy to grow. Many varieties are available. Smooth twigs have oval, glossy, deep green leaves. Flowers are $2^1/2$ to 4 inches wide and have single or double petals similar in shape to a rose or peony. They vary in color from white to deep rose-pink and dark red.

LANDSCAPE USE Popular as a specimen plant or planted as an informal hedge. Good to espalier against a sheltered wall. Good to grow under glass in colder climates.

BOTANICAL NAME *Campsis radicans*

COMMON NAME Trumpetcreeper; Trumpetvine; Hummingbird Vine

RANGE Zones 4–9. Native from Pennsylvania to Missouri, Florida to Texas.

HEIGHT 30 to 40 feet high; climbing vine.

CULTURE Rampant grower in any soil. Prefers full sun or partial shade. Prune back to a few buds in the spring. Propagated by seed.

DESCRIPTION Deciduous vine. Easy to grow. Two-and-a-half inch long, lustrous, dark green leaves change to yellow-green in the fall. Late leafer. Orange and scarlet trumpet-shaped flowers bloom on new growth from July to September. Fast grower (up to 10 feet per season) bursting with health and vitality.

LANDSCAPE USE Clings to wood, brick, and stucco surfaces with aerial rootlets. Good for screening. Use on trellises and lath structures. Attracts hummingbirds.

RECOMMENDED VARIETY 'Madame Galen', a hybrid cross between *C. radicans* and *C. grandiflora*.

BOTANICAL NAME *Carissa grandiflora*

COMMON NAME Natal-Plum

RANGE Zones 9–10. Native to South Africa.

HEIGHT 5 to 7 feet, but occasionally grows to 18 feet; low, spreading habit.

CULTURE Prefers well-drained, sandy or loam soil in full sun. Adapts to poor soil and to dry sites; will tolerate partial shade. Enjoys a warm south or west facing wall, preferably with an overhang to protect it from frost. Propagated by cuttings.

DESCRIPTION Broadleaf evergreen. Lustrous, leathery green leaves are 3 inches long. Fragrant white flowers are star-shaped, 2 inches wide. Flowers appear intermittently throughout the year, followed by red, plum-shaped, edible fruit.

LANDSCAPE USE Use as a low screen or hedge. Spines on stems discourage trespassers.

BOTANICAL NAME *Caryopteris* x *clandonensis*

COMMON NAME Blue-mist shrub; Bluebeard

RANGE Zones 6–9. Hybrid developed from species native to Asia.

HEIGHT 2 feet tall with equal spread; low-growing shrub.

CULTURE Prefers light, loamy, well-drained soil in full sun. Cut back nearly to the ground in spring to encourage new growth. Flowers grow only on new shoots. Propagated by cuttings.

DESCRIPTION Generally grown as a deciduous, shrubby perennial. Valued for its powder blue, mistylike flowers. Blooms August to frost. Leaves are medium green and narrow.

LANDSCAPE USE Lovely late-blooming garden shrub.

BOTANICAL NAME *Ceanothus thyrsiflorus*

COMMON NAME California Lilac; Blue Blossom Ceanothus

RANGE Zones 8–10. Native to western coastal ranges from Santa Barbara, California to southern Oregon.

HEIGHT Usually 4 to 8 feet tall; but sometimes seen as tall as 20 feet; bushy, spreading habit.

CULTURE Prefers well-drained, average garden soil in full sun. Drought tolerant. Propagated by cuttings.

DESCRIPTION Broadleaf evergreen shrub or small tree. Glossy, dark green leaves. Flowers bloom March or April and are light to dark blue, displayed in dense clusters.

LANDSCAPE USE Good specimen plant. Usually planted against a wall or fence.

BOTANICAL NAME *Celastrus scandens*

COMMON NAME American Bittersweet

RANGE Zones 3–8. Native to North America, including Canada.

HEIGHT 20 feet or higher; vine.

CULTURE Grows well in any soil in full sun. Needs both a male and female plant for fruit set. Propagated by seed and cuttings.

DESCRIPTION Vigorous and twining deciduous vine with ropelike branches. Needs strong support. Grown for yellow to orange fruit clusters, which split open revealing brilliant red-coated seeds inside. Flowers are white and bloom in June. Deep, glossy green leaves turn yellowish green in winter.

LANDSCAPE USE Use in poor soils on fences and old trees. Branches with fruit are popular for indoor winter arrangements. Considered a pest in some New England states. **Caution:** Fruit is poisonous.

BOTANICAL NAME *Cercis chinensis*

COMMON NAME Chinese Redbud; Chinese Judas-tree

RANGE Zone 6. Native to central China.

HEIGHT Less than 10 feet; multi-stemmed shrub.

CULTURE Adaptable to many well-drained soil types including acidic and alkaline soils, in full sun to light shade. Propagated by cuttings.

DESCRIPTION Deciduous. Showy, purple, pealike flowers, less than an inch long, bloom in March or April. New leaf growth emerges as reddish purple, changing to a dark, lustrous green in the summer. Fall color is yellow to yellowish green.

LANDSCAPE USE Attractive as a specimen plant, in groupings and in a shrub border.

BOTANICAL NAME *Chaenomeles speciosa*

COMMON NAME Flowering Quince

RANGE Zones 5–9. Native to China, Tibet, and Burma.

HEIGHT 6 to 10 feet high, 8 to 12 feet wide; mounded, bushy habit.

CULTURE Tolerant of most climatic conditions, although prefers an acidic soil in full sun. Blooms reluctantly in warm winter areas. Prune at any time to control shape or growth. Flowers bloom on new growth. Propagated by cuttings.

DESCRIPTION Deciduous. Grown primarily for the flowers that can be forced indoors as early as January. Flowers, ranging in color from white to pink to scarlet red, are up to 2 inches long, and bloom in early May. Occasional fragrant, yellowish, globe-shaped fruit appears in autumn. Shiny green leaves grow on thorny stems.

LANDSCAPE USE A popular, showy, flowering, deciduous shrub. Bare branches suggest an oriental look.

BOTANICAL NAME *Chamaecyparis pisifera*

COMMON NAME False Cypress

RANGE Zones 5–9. Native to Japan.

HEIGHT 20 to 30 feet with 20 feet spread; upright habit.

CULTURE Tolerant of a variety of conditions. However, plants dislike dry, alkaline, or heavy clay soils and strong, cold winds. Tolerates shade and pollution. Prune heavily to maintain a compact, tidy shape. Propagated by cuttings.

DESCRIPTION Narrowleaf evergreen. Loose, open growth with spiny, scale-like, rough leaves that are dark green above and lighter green below. Light bearer of cones.

LANDSCAPE USE Excellent in Oriental gardens. Good as a specimen plant, and in a foundation or boundary planting.

BOTANICAL NAME *Cistus ladanifer*

COMMON NAME Crimson-spot Rock-rose; Gum Rock-rose

RANGE Zone 7 south. Native to Mediterranean.

HEIGHT 3 to 5 feet tall; compact, shrubby habit.

CULTURE Prefers average, well-drained soil in full sun. Tolerates drought, poor, dry soil, cold ocean winds, sea spray, or desert heat. Pinch the tips of young plants to encourage thick growth. Propagated by seed and cuttings.

DESCRIPTION Deciduous leaves are 3 to 4 inches long, and are dark green above and whitish below. Fragrant, large, 3-inch wide white flowers have dark crimson spots at the base of the petals. Blooms in June and July.

LANDSCAPE USE Use as a dry bank cover, in rock gardens, along drives, and in mixed borders.

BOTANICAL NAME *Clematis* species and hybrids

COMMON NAME Clematis

RANGE Zones 3–9. Wild species are distributed mostly in North America and China.

HEIGHT 5 to 18 feet tall. Fast grower, up to 5 to 10 feet a year; vigorous vining habit.

CULTURE Mulch so that the roots stay cool while the tops are in partial shade or full sun. Plant in rich, loose, well-drained soil. Prefers a neutral to acidic soil. Varieties that bloom only in the spring should be pruned severely after flowering. Varieties that bloom in the summer, bloom only on new wood and should be cut back in the spring about 6 to 12 inches off the ground. Varieties that bloom in the spring and in the summer should be pruned lightly after flowering, as the blooms appear both on old and new wood. Propagated by seed and cuttings.

DESCRIPTION Deciduous. Not a difficult herbaceous vine to grow. Leaves are green. Flowers are 3 to 7 inches across and vary from white and pink to purple and blue.

LANDSCAPE USE Stems twist and twine around trellises, fences, walls, or any structure that offers a good support. Popular for covering arbors.

BOTANICAL NAME *Cornus florida*

COMMON NAME Flowering Dogwood

RANGE Zones 3–9. Native to North America.

HEIGHT 5 to 30 feet tall and to 30 feet wide; small tree.

CULTURE Deciduous. Easy to grow in neutral to acidic soil in sun or light shade. Tolerates pollution. To prevent anthracnose disease (also called lower branch dieback) keep plants watered during dry spells and feed by sprinkling a general purpose granular fertilizer around the drip line each spring. Propagated by cuttings.

DESCRIPTION Highly ornamental with white or pink star-shaped flowers, showy red fruit, and dramatic fall leaf colorings. Plants bloom in spring, outshining everything else in the garden. Fruit is favored by birds and squirrels. Pointed, oval green leaves have veins running parallel to the leaf margins. The autumn color varies among red, purple, and bronze foliage.

LANDSCAPE USE Excellent specimen tree to use as a lawn highlight. Popular for foundation plantings and as a canopy for mass plantings of azaleas.

BOTANICAL NAME *Cornus kousa*

COMMON NAME Korean dogwood

RANGE Zones 5–8. Native to Korea.

HEIGHT Up to 30 feet; mounded, spreading habit.

CULTURE Prefers humus-rich, acidic loam soil in full sun. Has better disease resistance than the native flowering dogwoods. Propagated from cuttings.

DESCRIPTION Deciduous. Spectacular flowering display similar to the native flowering dogwoods, except it blooms several weeks later, in early summer, and while the plant is in full leaf. The leaves are bright green, pointed, and serrated, and turn scarlet in autumn. Flowers are followed by edible fruits that resemble large raspberries.

LANDSCAPE USE Excellent lawn highlight and foundation accent. Exquisite planted as an avenue along a driveway.

BOTANICAL NAME *Cornus mas*

COMMON NAME Cornelian-cherry

RANGE Zones 5–9. Native to Europe and Asia.

HEIGHT 20 to 25 feet, equal spread; rounded habit.

CULTURE Easy to grow in any well-drained loam soil in full sun. Propagated mostly from cuttings. Transplant bare-root or from containers. Pollution resistant.

DESCRIPTION Small, deciduous tree valued for its yellow, early spring flowers, borne in clusters before the leaves appear. Leaves are oval, serrated, pointed, dark green. Oblong, cherry-red fruit appears in summer and is edible, generally eaten by birds as it ripens.

LANDSCAPE USE Good lawn highlight. Popular as an accent in beds and borders planted with daffodils and early-flowering perennials, such as pansies.

BOTANICAL NAME *Cornus sericea*

COMMON NAME Red-twig Dogwood

RANGE Zones 3-9. Native to North America.

HEIGHT Up to 8 feet, generally kept below 6 feet by pruning; erect habit.

CULTURE Tolerates a wide range of soil conditions, including wet soil, in full sun. Propagated by cuttings. Plant bare-root or from containers. Prune to the trunk after flowering to encourage a new set of juvenile stems.

DESCRIPTION Deciduous. Whiplike stems grow skyward. In the juvenile stage these are a brilliant red color and stand out as a beautiful ornamental accent in winter when the leaves have fallen. White flowers are borne in flat clusters, and appear soon after the leaves in spring. The bright green leaves are oval, pointed, and serrated, with prominent leaf veins typical of dogwoods.

LANDSCAPE USE Popular for massing on berms, raised mounds of soil built for screening. Good accent in mixed shrub borders and foundation plantings, especially planted against white stucco walls or white picket fences where the red winter bark color stands out dramatically.

BOTANICAL NAME *Corylopsis glabrescens*

COMMON NAME Fragrant Winterhazel

RANGE Zones 5–9. Native to China.

HEIGHT To 5 feet and as wide; mounded habit.

CULTURE Prefers well-drained, moist, acidic garden soil in partial shade or in a sheltered location in sun.

DESCRIPTION Deciduous. Valued for the soft yellow, fragrant flowers that bloom in March on bare stems. Dark green, oval-shaped leaves turn golden in the fall. Open, attractive, branching habit.

LANDSCAPE USE One of the earliest blooming shrubs. Branches are often cut and taken indoors in the spring to use in floral arrangements. Popular as a foundation shrub and as a winter accent in mixed shrub borders.

BOTANICAL NAME *Cotinus coggygria*

COMMON NAME Smoketree

RANGE Zones 5–8. Native to southern Europe and central China.

HEIGHT 10 to 15 feet with spread of 10 to 20 feet; upright, spreading, loose, open habit.

CULTURE Adaptable to a wide range of soil types in full sun. Readily transplanted. Can be pruned in March down to 5 to 6 feet to get a shrub effect. Propagated by seed and cuttings.

DESCRIPTION Deciduous. Brown or purplish bark with bluish green leaves. Ornamentally unimportant, small yellow flowers bloom in June and July. However, starting in July and lasting through September, clusters of flower stems burst into a spectacular show of soft, smokey pink hairs, resembling clouds hovering over the foliage. Small, kidney-shaped fruit develops after the show. Some varieties have purple leaves and purple flower stems.

LANDSCAPE USE Effective as a lawn accent and as a foundation plant.

BOTANICAL NAME *Cotoneaster horizontalis*

COMMON NAME Rock Spray

RANGE Zones 5–10. Native to China.

HEIGHT 3 to 4 feet high, spreading to 8 to 10 feet; low, spreading habit.

CULTURE Prefers well-drained soil in full sun. Likes good air circulation. Propagated by seed and cuttings.

DESCRIPTION Deciduous. Green, round, ¹/₂-inch long leaves turn a lovely bronze color in the fall. Branches spread by side shoots and give the overall appearance of a fish bone pattern. The early summer pink flowers are ornamentally unimportant but are followed by bright red berries that last through the fall, into the winter months.

LANDSCAPE USE Excellent ground cover that is often used in rock gardens to spill over boulders and retaining walls.

BOTANICAL NAME *Cytisus scoparius*

COMMON NAME Scotch Broom

RANGE Zones 5–8. Native to central and southern Europe.

HEIGHT 5 to 6 feet tall, spreading equal to or greater than height; bushy, mounded habit.

CULTURE Easy to grow, drought tolerant. Prefers well-drained garden soil in full sun. Propagated by seed or softwood cuttings.

DESCRIPTION Deciduous. Rounded shrub with upright, slender, medium green stems and twigs that keep their color throughout winter. Leaves are a light to medium green with no fall color. Bright yellow pea flowers bloom profusely on old wood in May and June. Fruit is a fuzzy brown pod of no ornamental importance.

LANDSCAPE USE Excellent plant for poor soil. Often seen dotting coastal highways. Good in mixed shrub borders and as a hedge plant.

BOTANICAL NAME *Daphne* x *burkwoodii*

COMMON NAME Burkwood Daphne

RANGE Zones 4–8. Wild species native to China.

HEIGHT 3 to 4 feet tall; mounded habit.

CULTURE Prefers well-drained, moist, slightly acidic to alkaline soil. Prefers some shade. Propagated by cuttings.

DESCRIPTION Tends to be semi-evergreen. Leaves are lustrous dark green above and lighter green beneath. The outstanding feature of this plant is the heavy, fragrant, pinkish white flower clusters that bloom in May. Flowers are followed by bright red berries, also borne in clusters.

LANDSCAPE USE Good in a shrub border, foundation planting, or near a walkway, where the fragrant flowers can be enjoyed.

BOTANICAL NAME *Deutzia gracilis*

COMMON NAME Slender Deutzia

RANGE Zones 4–8. Native to Japan.

HEIGHT 2 to 4 feet high, but can grow to 6 feet tall and 3 to 4 feet wide; compact, mounded habit.

CULTURE Prefers any good garden soil in full sun or very light shade. Transplant in the spring. Prune after flowering. Propagated by cuttings.

DESCRIPTION Deciduous. Graceful, wide-spreading, arching branches. Leaves are flat green in the summer, and turn slightly bronze in the fall. Flowers profusely in May in a mass of fragrant, white, star-shaped blooms.

LANDSCAPE USE A popular, easy-to-grow accent, hedge, or border plant.

BOTANICAL NAME *Enkianthus campanulatus*

COMMON NAME Redvein Enkianthus

RANGE Zones 4–7. Native to Japan.

HEIGHT 8 to 15 feet; upright, bushy habit.

CULTURE Prefers acidic soil in sun or partial shade. Propagated by seed or cuttings.

DESCRIPTION Deciduous. Beautiful, creamy yellow flowers resembling lily-of-the valley, are tinged orange or pink, appear in spring. Small, pointed, dark green leaves resemble azaleas, turn orange and red in autumn.

LANDSCAPE USE Good for foundation plantings, containers, bonsai, and hedges. Twiggy silhouette looks beautiful against winter landscape.

BOTANICAL NAME *Escallonia exoniensis*

COMMON NAME Escallonia

RANGE Zones 7–10. Native to South America.

HEIGHT Up to 10 feet, spreading 10 feet; dense, mounded habit.

CULTURE Prefers moist, acidic loam soil in full sun. Best planted from containers. Propagated by cuttings.

DESCRIPTION Weeping branches have dark green, heart-shaped leaves. Masses of small, rose-pink flowers cover the plant in spring.

LANDSCAPE USE Beautiful lawn highlight and billowing, informal hedge.

BOTANICAL NAME *Euonymus alata*

COMMON NAME Burning Bush; Winged Euonymus

RANGE Zones 4-7. Native to northeastern Asia and central China.

HEIGHT 7 to 10 feet high; 10 to 15 feet spread; mounded, bushy habit.

CULTURE Grows well in any well-drained soil in full sun to light shade. Propagated by cuttings.

DESCRIPTION Deciduous, dense shrub with side-spreading stiff branches that have corklike protrusions called "wings". Main interest comes in the fall when the medium- to deep green oval leaves turn a brilliant crimson so intense the plant seems to be on fire. If planted in partial shade the leaves turn a purplish red, never attaining their full, dazzling glory. Inconspicuous, tiny, greenish flower clusters bloom in May to be followed by a sparse crop of orange-red berries.

LANDSCAPE USE A popular plant with several seasons of interest. Stunning planted against dark evergreens. Use as background, screen, hedge, or specimen plant.

BOTANICAL NAME *Euonymus japonicus*

COMMON NAME Japanese Euonymus

RANGE Zones 7–9. Native to Japan.

HEIGHT 5 to 15 feet high, narrower in width. Prune for a low height; upright, shrubby habit.

CULTURE Adaptable to a variety of soils and conditions. Tolerates clay soil and ocean spray, and full sun to heavy shade. Propagated by division and cuttings.

DESCRIPTION Broadleaf evergreen. Attractive, deep green, glossy, leathery, oval leaves. Small, greenish white flowers appear in June, followed by pinkish orange berries. Varieties with variegated gold and silver leaves are offered.

LANDSCAPE USE Popular for its ability to grow well in unfavorable conditions. Effective as a hedge. Can be used as a houseplant.

BOTANICAL NAME *Exochorda racemosa*

COMMON NAME Pearlbush

RANGE Zones 5–9. Native to China.

HEIGHT 10 to 15 feet tall, spreading as wide; mounded, bushy habit.

CULTURE Grows well in almost any well-drained soil in full sun. Hard to establish in garden if planted bare-root. Buy as a container- grown plant or balled and burlapped. Prune off stem tips to maintain compact habit. Propagated by cuttings.

DESCRIPTION Deciduous. Although the flowers only last for about seven to twelve days in midspring, they are worth planting for the spectacular show of white, pearl-shaped buds that open into gorgeous flower clusters. Pointed, oval, attractive green leaves.

LANDSCAPE USE Use as a small specimen tree, or plant in groupings of three or more for an effective shrub border. Makes an attractive display planted against an evergreen background.

BOTANICAL NAME *Fatsia japonica*

COMMON NAME Japanese Aralia

RANGE Zones 8–10. Native to Japan.

HEIGHT Up to 10 feet; upright habit.

CULTURE Prefers moist, sandy, humus-rich soil in a lightly shaded location. Plant from containers. Propagated by cuttings.

DESCRIPTION Tender, evergreen shrub. Its large, handsome, figlike leaves give the plant a tropical appearance. Greenish yellow flower clusters occur in summer, enhancing the ornamental appearance of the leaves.

LANDSCAPE USE Mostly used in the southern United States and California to create a dramatic accent among foundation plantings, as well as in atriums and mixed shrub borders.

BOTANICAL NAME *Forsythia* x *intermedia*

COMMON NAME Forsythia

RANGE Zones 5–9. Hybrid cross from Germany.

HEIGHT 7 to 10 feet tall, with an equal spread; upright, arching, spreading habit.

CULTURE Accepts any well-drained soil condition in full sun or light shade. Propagated by seed and cuttings.

DESCRIPTION Deciduous. Grown for its prolific, deep yellow 1-inch flowers that bloom throughout March and April. The medium green leaves are long and somewhat oval shaped. In the fall, the foliage turns a yellow-green.

LANDSCAPE USE Valued for its early spring blooms. Effectively used in shrub borders, massings, groupings, and as a slope cover to control erosion.

RECOMMENDED VARIETY 'Lynwood Gold,' a mutation discovered in Ireland.

BOTANICAL NAME *Fothergilla gardenii*

COMMON NAME Dwarf Fothergilla

RANGE Zones 5-8. Native to Virginia and Georgia.

HEIGHT 2 to 3 feet high with similar or greater spread; upright, twiggy habit.

CULTURE Prefers well-drained, peaty, sandy, acidic soil in full sun or partial shade. Propagated by cuttings.

DESCRIPTION Deciduous. Can be difficult to establish. White fragrant flower spikes resemble pussy willows, burst into bloom on naked branches in April and May. Attractive dark green leaves are leathery and turn a brilliant yellow to orange-scarlet in the fall. Has a bare, twiggy, winter silhouette.

LANDSCAPE USE Good planted in combination with rhododendrons and azaleas. Excellent choice as an accent in tulip beds. Frequently used in foundation plantings, borders, and masses. Flowering stems are good for cutting to make attractive indoor floral arrangements.

BOTANICAL NAME *Fuchsia hybrida*

COMMON NAME Hybrid Fuchsia; Lady's Ear Drops

RANGE Zones 6–10. Native to South America.

HEIGHT 3 to 12 feet tall, depending upon variety; habit varies from erect shrub to trailing types.

CULTURE Prefers well-drained, humus-rich garden soil in partial shade. Enjoys cool summer temperatures where there is a lot of moisture and salt in the air, such as coastal locations. Prune by snipping off tips of branches to discourage legginess. Propagated by cuttings.

DESCRIPTION Fuchsias bloom from early summer to late frost. Over 500 varieties are grown, mostly on the West Coast of the United States. Flowers are mostly bicolored. The outer part of the flower is always white, red, or pink. The inner flower color can be any combination of white, blue-violet, purple, pink, red, and orange-red. The flowers are not fragrant. The green leaves are usually small, oval-shaped. Fuchsias wilt easily from lack of moisture and are prone to whiteflies and spider mites.

LANDSCAPE USE Makes an attractive hanging basket, and a small to large shrub, espalier, or standard form. Nectar of flowers is relished by hummingbirds.

BOTANICAL NAME *Gardenia jasminoides*

COMMON NAME Gardenia; Cape-jasmine

RANGE Zones 8–10. Native to China.

HEIGHT 3 to 5 feet tall with equal spread; mounded, bushy habit.

CULTURE Prefers a well-drained, moist, fertile, acidic soil in partial shade or full sun in coastal areas. Feed regularly with fertilizer during the growing season. Treat chlorosis with iron sulfate or iron chelate. Prune to remove faded blooms and wayward branches.

DESCRIPTION Broadleaf evergreen. Grown for its heavy fragrance and the beautiful, 3-inch wide, solitary, waxy white flowers which appear from late spring through summer. The glossy, thick, leathery, dark green leaves add to the overall beauty of the shrub. Intolerant of ocean spray.

LANDSCAPE USE Commonly used as a houseplant. Attractive in containers, raised beds, hedges, low screens, and as a specimen plant. Can be grown outdoors only in frost-free areas.

BOTANICAL NAME *Gelsemium sempervirens*

COMMON NAME Carolina Jessamine

RANGE Zones 6–9. Native to North America from Virginia to Florida.

HEIGHT 10 to 20 feet; vine.

CULTURE Prefers moist, well-drained, humus-rich soil in full sun, but will flower in partial shade. Propagated by seed and cuttings.

DESCRIPTION Broadleaf evergreen, twining vine. Shiny, bright green leaves are 1 to 4 inches long and run in pairs along thin, green to brown stems. Fragrant, tubular yellow flowers are 1 to 1½ inches long; bloom late winter through early spring.

LANDSCAPE USE Grows on trellises, stone walls, up small trees, and on fences and mailboxes. Can be used as a slope cover to control erosion. Will survive hard pruning to within 3 feet of the soil line to control its aggressive habit. **Caution:** All parts are highly poisonous.

BOTANICAL NAME *Hamamelis mollis*

COMMON NAME Chinese Witch-hazel

RANGE Zones 5–8. Native to China.

HEIGHT 10 to 15 feet tall with equal spread; rounded, sparse habit.

CULTURE Prefers moist, well-drained, acidic soil in full sun or partial shade. Temperatures below -15°F will cause damage. Propagated by seed or cuttings.

DESCRIPTION Deciduous. Ascending branches with soft, downy, new stems. Stark winter silhouette. The sweet, fragrant flower clusters are borne on naked stems and begin to bloom as early as January, through early March. The yellow flowers have a red base and are ½ inch wide. The 5-inch leaves are roundish, short, and pointed; medium green above and downy gray below. Leaves turn yellow in the fall.

LANDSCAPE USE Mainly planted for its early, fragrant bloom and its winter habit.

RECOMMENDED VARIETY 'Arnold's Promise,' a clear yellow.

BOTANICAL NAME *Hedera helix*

COMMON NAME English Ivy

RANGE Zones 5–10. Native to Europe and western Asia.

HEIGHT Up to 20 feet high; woody vine.

CULTURE Thrives in any good garden soil with average moisture in full sun. Propagated by cuttings.

DESCRIPTION Broadleaf evergreen. Thick, leathery, dark green leaves are lobed in the juvenile stage and smooth once adult. Some leaves may turn purplish in the fall in exposed areas. Small, greenish white flowers borne in clusters attract insects in the spring. In warm climates, black fruit is produced.

LANDSCAPE USE Terrific ground cover or climber. Ivy holds soil, discouraging erosion and slippage on slopes. Ivy tendrils cling to almost any vertical surface including walls, trellises, and fences. Also used in topiary designs.

BOTANICAL NAME *Hibiscus syriacus*

COMMON NAME Rose of Sharon; Shrub Althea

RANGE Zones 5–9. Native to China and India.

HEIGHT 6 to 20 feet tall and 8 to 10 feet wide; bushy, mounded habit.

CULTURE Prefers moist, fertile soil in full sun. Adaptable to most soil types and to partial shade in the hottest climates. Tolerates pollution and sea-shore conditions. Prune to maintain compact shape. Propagated by seed or cuttings.

DESCRIPTION Deciduous. Compact, much branched, and erect. Charming, hibiscus-like, unscented flowers, up to 3 inches across, bloom late July through August. Colors include white, red, purple, and blue with a crimson "eye." They can be single or double. Leaves are generally less than 3 inches long, oval-shaped, with a deep green to grayish green color. Drab autumn color.

LANDSCAPE USE Prune to a single trunk to make a small, flowering tree or sheer multiple trunks to make a screen or hedge. Well-grown specimens can produce masses of flowers to create a lawn highlight.

BOTANICAL NAME *Hydrangea macrophylla*

COMMON NAME Hydrangea

RANGE Zones 6–9. Native to Japan.

HEIGHT 5 to 8 feet tall, spreading 6 to 10 feet; symmetrical, rounded habit.

CULTURE Succeeds in any average soil in full sun or light shade. The blue to pink flower color is controlled by soil pH. Neutral or alkaline soil produces pink or red flowers. Acidic soil (prepare neutral or alkaline soils with aluminum sulfate) produces blue flowers. Tolerates seashore conditions. Propagated by cuttings.

DESCRIPTION Deciduous. Profuse bloomer in mild winter areas; likes the protection of a wall or fence where plants freeze to the ground in winter. The unscented, large, globular, lacy clusters of blue, pink, red, or white flowers bloom July through September and are reminiscent of flowers grown in an old-fashioned garden. Bright green leaves are oval-shaped, 4 to 8 inches long, with no fall color. Close to 400 cultivars are available.

LANDSCAPE USE Popular florist plant available around Easter and Mother's Day. Makes a good shrub border or accent plant.

RECOMMENDED VARIETY 'Annabelle,' a large-flowered, free-flowering, white variety.

BOTANICAL NAME *Hypericum calycinum*

COMMON NAME St.-John's-wort

RANGE Zones 4–8. Native to southeastern Europe and Asia Minor.

HEIGHT Up to 24 inches tall; dense, compact habit.

CULTURE Prefers well-drained, moist, loamy garden soil in full sun or partial shade. Tolerant of sandy soil. Invasive in good growing conditions. In colder climates needs protected site. Cut back any dead stems after new growth appears in early spring. Propagated by division or cuttings.

DESCRIPTION Evergreen except in colder climates. Grown for its prolific, glistening yellow flowers in mid- to late summer. Slender, oval, green leaves have conspicuous veins.

LANDSCAPE USE Versatile. Excellent ground cover. Good for erosion control on slopes. Desirable to use as a foundation planting near a house or as an edging to a shrub border.

RECOMMENDED VARIETY 'Hidcote'.

BOTANICAL NAME *Ilex* x *meserveae*

COMMON NAME Blue Holly; Meserve Hybrids

RANGE Zones 5–9. Hybrid cross developed in New York state.

HEIGHT 6 to 10 feet tall with equal width; upright habit.

CULTURE Prefers loose, well-drained, acidic soil in full sun or partial shade. Protect from wind in colder climates. Need both a male and a female plant to produce fruit. One male will pollinate up to eight females. Tip-prune to encourage new growth and maintain density. Propagated by cuttings.

DESCRIPTION Broadleaf evergreen. Valued for its beautiful, bluish green leaf tone. The glossy, leathery 2-inch leaves are wavy with spines. New stems have a purplish caste. Bright red fruit is persistent, remaining on the plant through autumn and winter. Generally more attractive than either American Holly (*I. opaca*) or English Holly (*I. aquifolia*), and bears more berries.

LANDSCAPE USE Excellent choice for hedges, foundation plantings, and as a lawn highlight. Can be pruned into cones to make sentinels on both sides of a gate or doorway. Attracts birds.

BOTANICAL NAME *Ilex verticillata*

COMMON NAME Winterberry

RANGE Zones 3–9. Native to swamps along the Eastern seaboard of North America.

HEIGHT 6 to 10 feet tall with equal spread; dense, multi-stemmed habit.

CULTURE Prefers moist, acidic, rich soil in full sun or partial shade. Tolerates light and heavy soils. Adaptable to wet conditions. Transplant balled and burlapped or as a container plant. Propagated by cuttings.

DESCRIPTION Broadleaf evergreen. Small, smooth, oval, dark green leaves are hairy below. Slender, angled, brown stems. Showy, bright red fruit appears August through January. Best to plant one male for every eight females in order to ensure a good berry display.

LANDSCAPE USE Choice plant along lakes and ponds where water can reflect fruit. In the winter, stunning as a mass planting where the red fruit contrasts against snowy lawns. Good foundation plant and lawn highlight. Attracts birds.

Left: One of the world's most beautiful topiary gardens is the Ladew Topiary Garden, near Monkton, Maryland. Here, whimsical figures are clipped out of an assortment of shrubs, including yew, boxwood, and hemlock.

BOTANICAL NAME *Juniperus horizontalis*

COMMON NAME Creeping Juniper

RANGE Zones 3–9. Native to North America.

HEIGHT 1 to 2 feet tall, spreading 4 to 8 feet; low, creeping habit.

CULTURE Prefers well-drained, stony or sandy, slightly alkaline soil in full sun. Tolerates exposure and hot, dry climates. Propagated by layering or cuttings.

DESCRIPTION Narrowleaf evergreen. Low-growing shrub with long trailing branches forming large mats. Leaves vary from green to steel blue, depending on the variety, with a purplish caste in the winter. Flowers and cones are ornamentally unimportant.

LANDSCAPE USE A popular, low ground cover that persists in poor situations, including seashore plantings. Good slope cover to control erosion. Effective for rock gardens and as an edging to foundation plantings.

BOTANICAL NAME *Kalmia latifolia*

COMMON NAME Mountain-laurel

RANGE Zones 4–9. Native to eastern North America.

HEIGHT 4 to 8 feet; upright, bushy habit.

CULTURE Prefers cool, moist, well-drained, acidic soil in full sun or partial shade. Flowers best in full sun, but one of the best flowering shrubs for deep shade. Easy to transplant. Mulch to keep soil moist. Propagated by cuttings.

DESCRIPTION Broadleaf evergreen. Slow-grower. In youth, symmetrical and loose; old age, open with gnarled trunks and limbs. One-half-inch hexagonal-shaped flowers are borne in large, showy clusters up to 5 inches across. Colors include white, pink, red, and purple. The buds, too, are extremely attractive, folded in intricate patterns. Two-to-5 inch leathery, dark green leaves arranged in a whorl. Brown seed capsules last throughout the winter, but are best removed before they develop seeds to encourage flowering for the next season.

LANDSCAPE USE One of the best-loved native flowering shrubs. Excellent for naturalizing. Good specimen for shady borders and mass plantings.

BOTANICAL NAME *Kerria japonica*

COMMON NAME Japanese Kerria

RANGE Zones 4–9. Native to China.

HEIGHT 5 to 8 feet, 6 to 9 feet wide; spreading habit.

CULTURE Prefers loamy, well-drained soil of moderate fertility in full shade. Transplant balled and burlapped or from a container. Prune away any dead branches. Propagated by cuttings.

DESCRIPTION Deciduous. Densely branched and twiggy with yellowish to bright green stems that spread by suckering. Bright green leaves turn yellow in the fall. The golden yellow, single, cup-shaped flowers bloom April through May, and are ½ to 2 inches across. The variety 'Pleniflora' has double flowers.

LANDSCAPE USE Tough plant. Effective as an informal hedge. Tolerates light shade and for this reason plants look good massed in a woodland garden.

BOTANICAL NAME *Kolkwitzia amabilis*

COMMON NAME Beauty Bush

RANGE Zones 5–8. Native to China.

HEIGHT 7 to 15 feet high and 5 to 10 feet wide; erect, dense, compact habit.

CULTURE Prefers well-drained loam soil in full sun or partial shade. Easy to grow. Propagated by cuttings.

DESCRIPTION Deciduous. Graceful, many-branched, fountainlike shrub. Dark green leaves are fuzzy and turn a dull red in autumn. The 3-inch flower clusters bloom profusely in late May. The bell-shaped flowers are bright pink with yellow throats. Tiny, hairy seed heads are noticeable in late June. Decorative brown bark peels in large strips and flakes on older stems.

LANDSCAPE USE Good screen or border plant. Excellent lawn highlight and foundation specimen.

BOTANICAL NAME *Lagerstroemia indica*

COMMON NAME Crape-myrtle

RANGE Zones 7–10. Native to China and Korea.

HEIGHT 12 to 20 feet tall, 8 to 12 feet wide; tree-like habit.

CULTURE Prefers a moist, well-drained, rich organic soil in full sun. Tolerates dry, poor soil, pollution, and extreme heat. Transplant when balled and burlapped or from a container. Propagated by cuttings.

DESCRIPTION Deciduous. Dense shrub can develop into a small, flowering tree. Bud clusters, 6 to 12 inches long, burst into wrinkled, 1-inch, pink, purple, or white flowers resembling lilacs. Young leaves are bronze, maturing to medium or dark green. Vivid show of orange, red, and yellow fall color. Attractive, smooth, brownish gray bark peels to reveal maroon and pinkish blotches.

LANDSCAPE USE Use as a lawn accent and to create an avenue framing a path. Suitable for planting in containers. Extremely popular in hot climates because it is heat and drought resistant.

BOTANICAL NAME *Lantana camara*

COMMON NAME Shrub Verbena; Common Lantana

RANGE Zones 8–10. Native to the West Indies.

HEIGHT To 6 feet; upright, spreading habit.

CULTURE Tolerates any well-drained garden soil. Excess water and fertilizer inhibits blooms. Prune in spring to remove dead wood and to maintain a compact habit. Propagated by cuttings.

DESCRIPTION Vining shrub grown for profuse, all-year bloom in frost-free areas. Rough, dark green leaves. One-to-2-inch flower clusters bloom yellow, orange, or red.

LANDSCAPE USE Use for low hedges and foundation plantings. An extremely versatile plant that can be sheared to keep it low and bushy, or trained to climb up a trellis. In areas with severe winters, it is often grown in pots, pruned to a single trunk, and moved indoors.

BOTANICAL NAME *Leucothoe fontanesiana*

COMMON NAME Drooping Leucothoe

RANGE Zones 4–6. Native to mid-Atlantic and southeastern United States.

HEIGHT 3 to 6 feet tall with equal spread; spreading, arching habit.

CULTURE Prefers loose, moist, well-drained, acidic, high-organic soil in partial shade. Protect from full sun and wind. Propagated by seed or cuttings.

DESCRIPTION Broadleaf evergreen. Majestic, long, arching, leathery green leaves stir with the slightest breeze. Leaves turn bronze in the fall. Fragrant, white, pendulous flowers bloom in May.

LANDSCAPE USE All season interest. Excellent cover for banks or cascading over retaining walls. An interesting, graceful plant for massing along woodland walks and driveways. Contrasts well with rhododendrons.

BOTANICAL NAME *Ligustrum* x *vicaryi*

COMMON NAME Vicary Golden Privet

RANGE Zones 6–10. Native to England.

HEIGHT 3 to 12 feet tall, 4 to 15 feet wide; dense, rounded habit.

CULTURE Adaptable to a variety of soils in full sun or partial shade. Its coloring is more effective in sun. Propagated by cuttings.

DESCRIPTION Deciduous. Slow-growing. Leaves are green with an overlay of bright gold or yellow-green if planted in a shady area. Small, white clusters of flowers bloom in July and are ornamentally unimportant.

LANDSCAPE USE Attractive specimen for a shrub border. Good container plant. Makes an unusual hedge, especially when alternated with a regular green privet for a "checkered" effect.

BOTANICAL NAME *Lonicera japonica* 'Halliana'

COMMON NAME Japanese Honeysuckle

RANGE Zones 5–10. Native to Japan.

HEIGHT To 15 feet tall; vine.

CULTURE Adaptable to any soil in sun or shade. Tolerates poor drainage. Prune back almost to the ground once a year to keep plants bushy. Propagated by cuttings.

DESCRIPTION Evergreen to wholly deciduous in coldest regions. Rampant grower. Oval green leaves. Sweet, fragrant white flowers that change to yellow or take on a purplish tinge, are borne in profusion in early summer.

LANDSCAPE USE Good climber that is used for bank and ground cover. Effective for erosion control. Train on screen or fence. Somewhat invasive if not kept within bounds. Plants that escape into the wild can suffocate small trees.

BOTANICAL NAME *Magnolia stellata*

COMMON NAME Star Magnolia

RANGE Zones 3-8. Native to Japan.

HEIGHT 15 to 20 feet tall with spread of 15 feet; compact, wide spreading habit.

CULTURE Prefers peaty, highly rich soil in full sun or light shade. Flowers are injured by frost. Transplant balled and burlapped or from containers. Propagated by cuttings.

DESCRIPTION Deciduous. Slow-growing. Low-branched, multi-stemmed shrub that can be trained into a tree. White, many petaled, fragrant, star-shaped flowers bloom in early April. Thick green leaves turn yellow to bronze in autumn. Bark is smooth, gray.

LANDSCAPE USE Pointed, downy flower buds add interest during winter months. Excellent single specimen or accent plant. Good integrated into foundation plantings.

BOTANICAL NAME *Myrica cerifera*

COMMON NAME Southern Wax-myrtle

RANGE Zones 7–10. Native from New Jersey to Florida and west to Texas.

HEIGHT 35 feet tall, 20 feet wide; open habit.

CULTURE Prefers moist, peaty, or wet, sandy soil in full sun. Transplants easily. Good seashore plant. Propagated by cuttings.

DESCRIPTION Deciduous. Clump-forming shrub grown for its waxy, fragrant, green, narrow leaves; and for its fragrant, waxy, gray-green fruit. Flowers are ornamentally unimportant. Easy to grow.

LANDSCAPE USE Good border plant. Often used in seashore plantings. The berried branches are beautiful used in both fresh and dried winter floral arrangements.

BOTANICAL NAME *Nandina domestica*

COMMON NAME Heavenly-bamboo; Nandina

RANGE Zones 6–9. Native to China.

HEIGHT 6 to 8 feet tall; upright, loose habit.

CULTURE Prefers loose, well-drained, moist, fertile soil in full sun or partial shade. Spreads by rhizomes. Propagated by cuttings.

DESCRIPTION Deciduous. Overall oriental appearance. Open, fine-textured, 2-inch long leaves are arranged in threes on slender stems resembling bamboo. Autumn foliage is plum-red. Clusters of white flowers bloom in summer. Handsome, bright red berries appear August through October and last well into winter.

LANDSCAPE USE Mainly used as a screen, background, and foundation planting. Can be grown as a container plant. Effective under deciduous trees like oak and maple. Dwarf forms are suitable as a ground cover. The generous berry clusters make beautiful holiday decorations and arrangements.

Right: Beautiful evergreen pieris, planted beneath the flowering branches of a dogwood, help form a corridor along a flagstone path. Rhododendrons and hemlock are also featured in this verdant planting.

BOTANICAL NAME *Nerium oleander*

COMMON NAME Oleander

RANGE Zones lower 8–10. Native to Southern Asia and the Mediterranean region.

HEIGHT 6 to 20 feet tall with equal spread; upright, rounded, bushy habit.

CULTURE Prefers well-drained, loam or sandy soil in sun or partial shade. Tolerant of seashore and dry conditions and pollution. Transplants easily. Propagated by cuttings.

DESCRIPTION Broadleaf evergreen, rapid-growing, many branched shrub. Large, leathery, pointy, dark gray-green leaves can grow up to 10 inches long. Pretty, fragrant, single or double flowers borne in clusters, bloom from June to August. Color range includes white, pink, and red.

LANDSCAPE USE Effective as a tall hedge, massed for erosion control, and in border, screen, and foundation plantings. In Northern states and other areas with freezing winter temperatures, plants are grown in containers so that they can be moved indoors. **Caution:** All parts are poisonous if eaten.

BOTANICAL NAME *Osmanthus heterophyllus*

COMMON NAME Holly Osmanthus

RANGE Zones 7–9. Native to China.

HEIGHT 8 to 10 feet tall with similar spread; dense, spreading habit.

CULTURE Prefers moist, well-drained, rich, acidic soil in full sun. Will withstand heavy pruning. Propagated by cuttings.

DESCRIPTION Broadleaf evergreen. Grown for its lustrous, dark green, spiny leaves. Heavily scented white flowers bloom September through November and are hidden by foliage.

LANDSCAPE USE Use as an elegant, formal specimen planted near walkways. Also effective as a screen, barrier, or hedge. Similar in appearance to holly, capable of being trimmed into cones and mounded shapes.

BOTANICAL NAME *Paeonia suffruticosa*

COMMON NAME Tree Peony

RANGE Zones 5–8. Native to China.

HEIGHT 3 to 6 feet high, up to 12 feet across; loose, mounded habit.

CULTURE Prefers a well-drained, moist, rich soil in a sheltered position. Likes its feet in the shade and its head in the sun, though it will tolerate partial shade. Propagated by cuttings.

DESCRIPTION Deciduous. Beautiful, maple-shaped leaves and huge single or double flowers up to 10 inches across make this one of the most spectacular of all flowering shrubs. Color range includes white, yellow, pink, red, crimson, and purple to almost black, all with a prominent, powdery yellow crest of stamens in the center.

LANDSCAPE USE A good family of plants to collect, planted spontaneously throughout the garden as lawn accents, in mixed shrub borders, and as a foundation planting.

BOTANICAL NAME *Parthenocissus quinquefolia*

COMMON NAME Virginia Creeper

RANGE All zones. Native to North America.

HEIGHT Up to 30 feet; tall, vigorous vine.

CULTURE Prefers well-drained, moist loam soil in full sun or partial shade.

DESCRIPTION Deciduous. Clinging vine that attaches itself to walls and other structures by its tendrils. Grown for its beautiful orange to scarlet fall leaf color. Leaves are saw-toothed, lustrous green in summer, divided into five leaflets. Difficult to remove once established. Looser habit than Boston ivy, to which it is closely related.

LANDSCAPE USE Good vine for covering walls and tall structures. Use as a ground cover on slopes.

BOTANICAL NAME *Philadelphus coronarius*

COMMON NAME Sweet Mock-orange

RANGE Zones 5–8. Native to southeastern Europe and Asia Minor.

HEIGHT 7 to 10 feet and as wide; rounded habit.

CULTURE Prefers well-drained, moist, rich soil in full sun or partial shade. Tolerates dry conditions. Prune after flowering to prevent legginess. Propagated by seed or cuttings.

DESCRIPTION Vigorous, erect, and dense with oval, dark green leaves, 2 to 3 inches long. Leaf stalks are hairy. Grown for its fragrant clusters of 1- to 1½-inch wide white flowers that appear in early June. Both single and double forms are available.

LANDSCAPE USE An old-fashioned favorite as a lawn accent and reliable foundation plant. Good to create informal screens and windbreaks.

BOTANICAL NAME *Photinia* x *fraseri*

COMMON NAME Fraser Photinia; Red Tips

RANGE Zones 7–10. Originated in Alabama through hybridizing.

HEIGHT 20 feet high and half as wide; upright, bushy habit.

CULTURE Prefers well-drained, rich, loam soil in full sun or partial shade. Intolerant to wet soils. Transplants easily. Takes heavy pruning. Propagated by cuttings.

DESCRIPTION Broadleaf evergreen. Vigorous. Grown for its bright coppery red new foliage. The slender, pointed mature leaves are glossy and dark green. Clusters of white flowers bloom in the spring.

LANDSCAPE USE Stunning hedge or container plant. Good lawn highlight. Also can be espaliered.

BOTANICAL NAME *Picea pungens nana*

COMMON NAME Dwarf Blue Spruce

RANGE Zones 3–8. Native to Wyoming, Utah, Colorado, and New Mexico.

HEIGHT 3 to 5 feet tall; densely pyramidal habit.

CULTURE Prefers moderately rich, well-drained, gravelly soil in full sun. Tolerates dry and moist soil. Propagated by cuttings.

DESCRIPTION Slow-growing narrowleaf evergreen. Rigid, horizontal branching. Grown for its adaptability. Sharp $1/2$- to $1\,1/4$- inch gray to gray-green needles adorn this prickly plant. Shiny, oblong cones are 2 to 4 inches long.

LANDSCAPE USE Good seashore plant. Excellent planted near a house or in a rock garden. If regularly pruned, it can be shaped into mounds and made into a low hedge.

BOTANICAL NAME *Pieris japonica*

COMMON NAME Japanese Andromeda

RANGE Zones 5–8. Native to Japan.

HEIGHT 9 to 12 feet high with 6 to 8 feet spread; upright, dense habit.

CULTURE Prefers loose, moist, well-drained, acidic soil in full sun or partial shade. Shelter from winds. Prune after flowering to maintain a compact habit. Transplant balled and burlapped or as a container plant. Propagated by cuttings.

DESCRIPTION Broadleaf evergreen. Bushy habit with spreading branches and rosettelike foliage. New leaves are a rich bronze which change to a lustrous, dark green at maturity. Large, drooping clusters of slightly fragrant, white, urn-shaped flowers bloom March through April. Flower buds add winter appeal since they are formed the summer prior to flowering.

LANDSCAPE USE Excellent lawn specimen or foundation plant. Effective in shrub borders mixed with other broadleaf evergreens, such as azaleas and rhododendrons.

BOTANICAL NAME *Pinus mugo*

COMMON NAME Mugo Pine, Swiss Mountain Pine

RANGE Zones 2–7. Native to central and southern Europe from Spain to the Balkans.

HEIGHT 15 to 20 feet with 25 to 30 feet spread; low-spreading or pyramidal habit.

CULTURE Prefers moist loam soil in sun or partial shade. Transplant balled and burlapped or buy container plants. Prune to thicken plant and to keep a dwarf habit. Propagated by seed and cuttings.

DESCRIPTION Narrowleaf evergreen. Slow-growing, variable plants. Mostly forms a low, mounded shape. Needles vary in color from medium green in summer to yellowish green in winter. The grayish brown, 1- to 2-inch cones stand erect.

LANDSCAPE USE Best used in groups of three or more plants as a dwarf planting in foundations and rock gardens.

BOTANICAL NAME *Pittosporum tobira*

COMMON NAME Japanese Pittosporum

RANGE Zones 8–10. Native to Japan, Formosa, Korea, and China.

HEIGHT 6 to 12 feet high and 4 to 5 feet wide; dense, broad-spreading habit.

CULTURE Prefers any well-drained soil in full sun or shade. Enjoys dry locations. Tolerates salt spray. Easy to transplant. Tip-prune to encourage bushiness or to control height. Propagated by cuttings.

DESCRIPTION Broadleaf evergreen. Lustrous, blunt, wide, dark green leaves are set in whorls on brown stems. When crushed, leaves produce a disagreeable odor. Creamy white to yellow fragrant flower clusters open in April and May. Green, pear-shaped fruit turns to brown at maturity in September and October.

LANDSCAPE USE Popular in mass plantings, foundations, and as drifts under trees. Suitable for hedges, screens, and barrier plantings. Interesting container plant. Foliage used in both fresh and dried floral arrangements.

BOTANICAL NAME *Podocarpus macrophyllus*

COMMON NAME Yew Podocarpus

RANGE To 50 feet tall; stiff, upright habit.

HEIGHT Zones 8–10. Native to Japan, southern China.

CULTURE Prefers well-drained, loam or sandy garden soil in full sun or partial shade. Tolerant of salt spray. Easily pruned to form a column shape. Propagated by cuttings.

DESCRIPTION Narrowleaf evergreen. Versatile plant with good-looking foliage. Lustrous, dark green, narrow leaves. Flowers bloom in April and May, followed by small, edible, bluish fruit.

LANDSCAPE USE Grows indoors and out in tubs and open ground. Use for espalier, screen plantings, topiary, and clipped hedges. A popular street tree in warm climates.

BOTANICAL NAME *Poncirus trifoliata*

COMMON NAME Hardy-orange

RANGE Zones 6–9. Native to Northern China and Korea.

HEIGHT 10 to 15 feet tall with almost equal spread; oval-shaped, twiggy habit.

CULTURE Prefers a well-drained, acidic soil in full sun. Easily transplanted. Propagated by seed or cuttings.

DESCRIPTION Deciduous. Low-branching shrub or small tree with green, sharp spines. Young bark is green; older bark is slightly furrowed. Oval leaves are light green and are in sets of threes. Foliage turns to yellow in autumn. Fragrant, white, single flowers are 1 to 2 inches across, resemble orange-blossoms and appear in April and May. Attractive, small, downy, yellow, golf-ball-sized fruit appears in September and October. Extremely fragrant. Fruit is highly astringent, remains on the tree a short time after the leaves have dropped.

LANDSCAPE USE Effective for screen, privacy, and security. Use as a hedge or a barrier plant. Unusual, high interest plant suitable for containers and foundation accent.

BOTANICAL NAME *Potentilla fruticosa*

COMMON NAME Bush Cinquefoil

RANGE Zones 2–8. Native to Europe and Asia.

HEIGHT 2 to 4 feet high with equal spread; rounded habit.

CULTURE Adaptable to dry and wet soil, also heavy and sandy soil in full sun to light shade. Drought tolerant. Propagated by cuttings.

DESCRIPTION Hardy, deciduous, dense shrub that has a fine-textured appearance. The long-stalked, bright green leaves consist of five oval leaflets about ½ inch long. Flowers are creamy white to bright yellow and look like miniature, single-flowered roses. They bloom intermittently, starting in late May. Bark is flaky and deep brown.

LANDSCAPE USE Good for ground covers and accents in borders. Pink- and red-flowering varieties are available, but these tend to be plants suitable only for areas with cool, moist summers, such as the Pacific Northwest.

BOTANICAL NAME *Prunus glandulosa* 'Alboplena'

COMMON NAME Flowering Almond

RANGE Zones 4–8. Native to China and Japan.

HEIGHT 3 to 5 feet tall with equal spread; upright habit.

CULTURE Prefers well-drained, moist, humus-rich soil in full sun. Prune after flowering to increase new stem development. Propagated by cuttings.

DESCRIPTION Deciduous. Somewhat rounded shrub with slender, multistems. The most popular variety, 'Rosea,' has lovely 1-inch double flowers crowded along the stems like pink powderpuffs, appearing in early spring. Foliage is oval, light green, and provides no autumn interest.

LANDSCAPE USE Specimen shrub used for flowering display in mixed borders. Popular for planting in the middle of tulip displays and beds of early perennials, such as pansies, to provide a spectacular color highlight.

BOTANICAL NAME *Pyracantha coccinea*

COMMON NAME Scarlet Firethorn

RANGE Zones 6–9. Native to Italy and the Caucausus mountain region.

HEIGHT 6 feet high and 10 feet wide; erect habit.

CULTURE Prefers well-drained, sandy or loam soil in full sun or partial shade. Difficult to transplant. Propagated by seeds or cuttings. Plants are susceptible to fireblight disease, a bacteria that turns the fruit black as if scorched.

DESCRIPTION Broadleaf evergreen. Open shrub with stiff, thorny branches. Lustrous, dense, dark green leaves may turn brown during winter in unprotected areas. Malodorous, profuse, white, showy flowers bloom in April and June. Spectacular, orange-red berry-like fruit persists through the winter.

LANDSCAPE USE Grown primarily for showy fruit. Use as an informal hedge or barrier plant. Good for espaliers on walls and trellises. Some varieties have yellow berries.

BOTANICAL NAME *Raphiolepis indica*

COMMON NAME Indian Hawthorn; India Raphiolepis

RANGE Zones 7–10. Native to Japan and Korea.

HEIGHT 4 to 5 feet high with equal spread; dense, mounded habit.

CULTURE Prefers well-drained loam soil in full sun. Tolerates occasional drought, and seashore conditions. Prune after flowering to retain shape. Propagated by seed and cuttings.

DESCRIPTION Broadleaf evergreen. Spectacular show of flowers from late fall through mid-winter. Colors range from white to a light red. Attractive dark blue berries follow, persisting through winter. New leaves in tones of bronze and red also add ornamental interest. Adult foliage is glossy, dark green, and pointed. Habit can be sturdy, bushy, and compact or a natural spreading, open shape.

LANDSCAPE USE A great basic landscape shrub. Makes a good, dense mass planting, large-scale ground cover, low divider, or informal hedge. Especially popular in drought-prone areas.

Left: Beautiful blue spruce provides a spectacular contrast to the heather and ornamental grasses in this hillside garden.

BOTANICAL NAME *Rhododendron* species (Azalea)

COMMON NAME Azalea

RANGE Zones 1–10. Native to China and Japan, also North America.

HEIGHT Generally 2 to 15 feet high and 3 to 9 feet wide, depending on variety; rounded, spreading habit.

CULTURE Prefers well-drained, moist, rich, acidic soil in partial shade or full sun in cool summer areas. Protect from strong, cold winds. Tolerates air pollution. Easy to transplant. Tip-prune plant after bloom period to maintain compact habit. Propagated by seed and cuttings.

DESCRIPTION Azaleas are really rhododendrons, but differ from the generally accepted notion of a rhododendron in having smaller leaves and flowers, and a more compact, low-spreading habit. Mostly deciduous but some species are evergreen. Flowers are generally funnel-shaped, in white, pink, red, purple, yellow, and orange. Prime bloom time is from spring to early summer. The leathery leaves are rounded, smooth-edged, and set in whorls. Leaves are frequently hairy.

LANDSCAPE USE Attractive, versatile plant. Perfect for shrub borders, groupings, massings, and foundation plantings.

BOTANICAL NAME *Salix discolor*

COMMON NAME Pussy Willow

RANGE Zones 2–9. Native to the eastern United States.

HEIGHT To 20 feet tall; upright, twiggy habit.

CULTURE Prefers moist, humus-rich soil in full sun. Readily transplanted. Propogated by cuttings.

DESCRIPTION Deciduous. Fast-grower with invasive roots. Slender, brownish red stems with 2- to 4-inch oval leaves that are bright green above, and bluish below. Beloved for their soft, silky, pearl-gray flowers called catkins that measure up to 1$\frac{1}{2}$ inches long on the male plants.

LANDSCAPE USE Old-fashioned favorite. Plant as a single specimen or combine it with other plants in borders. Branches may easily be forced for indoor winter bloom. Keep plants pruned hard so flowering branches are always easily within reach.

BOTANICAL NAME *Skimmia japonica*

COMMON NAME Japanese Skimmia

RANGE Zones 6–9. Native to Japan.

HEIGHT 1 to 5 feet tall with similar spread; mounded, dense habit.

CULTURE Prefers loose, moist, well-drained, humus-rich acidic soil in partial shade. Propagated by seed and cuttings.

DESCRIPTION Broadleaf evergreen. Flower sexes are on separate plants. Male plant is smaller and can service about a dozen female plants for berry production. The purple-red buds open to sweetly scented, creamy white flowers in March and April. In October, festive, bright red clusters of berries appear on the female plants. Leaves are green above, lighter green below, oblong, and smooth.

LANDSCAPE USE Beautiful, dainty evergreen shrub. Use as a ground cover, in foundation plantings, or planter boxes. Also popular in rock gardens.

BOTANICAL NAME *Spiraea* x *vanhouttei*

COMMON NAME Bridalwreath; Vanhoutte Spirea

RANGE Zones 5–10. Developed from species native to China.

HEIGHT 6 to 8 feet tall and 8 to 10 feet wide; fountainlike habit.

CULTURE Tolerant of many fertile soils in full sun. Easy to transplant. Propagated by cuttings.

DESCRIPTION Deciduous. Graceful, round-topped, arching branches fall to the ground, giving a broad, mounded appearance. Fast-growing and durable. Leaves are a dull bluish green with grayish undersides. Some slight autumn leaf color ranging from red to orange. The showy white flower clusters bloom in April and May.

LANDSCAPE USE Widely used as a lawn highlight, hedge, or screen planting.

BOTANICAL NAME *Syringa vulgaris*

COMMON NAME Lilac

RANGE Zones 3–7. Native to the Balkan penninsula.

HEIGHT 8 to 15 feet tall and 6 to 12 feet wide; upright habit.

CULTURE Prefers a moist, humus-rich, neutral soil in full sun. Prune to revitalize overgrown or damaged plants. Propagated by cuttings.

DESCRIPTION Deciduous. Grown for the pleasant, gratifying fragrance of its flowers, which appear mid-May to early June, in dense, erect clusters of lavender-blue, purple, red, and white. The almost bluish green leaves are semi-glossy and heart-shaped.

LANDSCAPE USE An old-fashioned favorite. As the seasonal interest is limited to length of bloom time, plant sparingly. Use in a shrub border or in foundation plantings. The flowers make exquisite indoor arrangements.

BOTANICAL NAME *Tamarix ramosissima*

COMMON NAME Tamarix; Five Stamen Tamarisk

RANGE Zone 2 south. Native to southeastern Europe and central Asia.

HEIGHT 10 to 15 feet tall with narrower spread; loose, open habit.

CULTURE Prefers well-drained, acidic soil in full sun. Tolerates sandy soil and seashore conditions. Easy to grow. Propagated by seed and cuttings.

DESCRIPTION Deciduous. Fast-growing, spreading shrub with attractive, bright green, feathery foliage. The dense clusters of tiny, pale pink flowers bloom June through July.

LANDSCAPE USE Grown primarily for its adaptability to saline environments. Use in mixed plantings, such as mixed shrub borders, and along the side of a wall or fence where its arching stems and light, airy flower clusters can cascade over the top.

BOTANICAL NAME *Taxus cuspidata*

COMMON NAME Japanese Yew

RANGE Zones 4–7. Native to Japan, Korea, and Manchuria.

HEIGHT 50 feet high, spreading 25 feet wide; upright habit.

CULTURE Prefers well-drained loam soil in full sun or part shade. Tolerant of both drought and cold. Propagated by cuttings.

DESCRIPTION Rapid-growing, hardy, narrowleaf evergreen. Can reach tree size but usually remains a sturdy, multi-stemmed shrub. Twigs are yellow-green with broad, leathery, 1¼-inch dull green needles, with conspicuous, yellow-green undersides. Leaves form a distinct V-shaped pattern as they lay flat in two rows along the stem. Stem bark is reddish to grayish brown and flakes off with age. Oval red berries appear in autumn.

LANDSCAPE USE The tall varieties make good accents as sentinels to doorways and garden entrances. Also valuable as a hedge. Dwarf, spreading kinds can be sheared into mounds.

BOTANICAL NAME *Trachelospermum jasminoides*

COMMON NAME Star or Confederate Jasmine; Chinese Star-jasmine

RANGE Zones 7–9. Native to China.

HEIGHT To 20 feet tall; vine.

CULTURE Prefers well-drained, moist loam soil in full sun or partial shade in hottest areas. Once established it grows moderately fast. Prune to hold shape. Cut back older plants by one-third each year to spruce up plant. Propagated by cuttings.

DESCRIPTION Broadleaf evergreen, sprawling vine. The lustrous, dark green leaves are 3 inches long. The clusters of sweetly fragrant white flowers bloom profusely in June and July.

LANDSCAPE USE Can be trained as a spreading shrub or ground cover. Mostly used as a decorative vine to camouflage walls and fences. Suitable for containers or trained up a short trellis.

BOTANICAL NAME *Tsuga canadensis* 'Sargentii'

COMMON NAME Weeping Hemlock

RANGE Zones 3–7. Native to eastern United States.

HEIGHT 2 to 3 feet high and twice as wide; low, broad habit.

CULTURE Prefers moist, acidic soil with high humidity in partial shade. Protect from hot sun and wind. Propagated by layering, seed, and cuttings.

DESCRIPTION Narrowleaf evergreen. Drooping branches with flat, narrow needles are dark green above and white-banded below. Small, oval, brown cones hang from branches in autumn.

LANDSCAPE USE Excellent plant to use as an accent in large rock gardens. Can look sensational as a lawn highlight. The branches and leaves seem to cascade like a waterfall.

BOTANICAL NAME *Viburnum opulus sterile*

COMMON NAME European Snowball Bush

RANGE Zones 3–8. Native to Europe, northern Africa, and northern Asia.

HEIGHT 8 to 12 feet tall and 10 to 15 feet wide; upright, spreading habit.

CULTURE Prefers well-drained loam soil in full sun, but tolerates boggy soil. Propagated by seed and cuttings.

DESCRIPTION Deciduous. Maple-shaped leaves, 2 to 4 inches long, are dark green and glossy. Inconsistent fall coloring, but when the leaves turn, they range from yellow-red to a reddish purple. The immature flower clusters are green before turning globular and white, thus resembling snowballs; they bloom during the month of May.

LANDSCAPE USE Grown for its showy flower display. Use in shrub borders and as a screen. Popular for planting against low fences and walls so the heavily laden flowering stems can spill over the top.

BOTANICAL NAME *Vinca minor*

COMMON NAME Periwinkle; Myrtle

RANGE Zones 4–9. Native to northeastern United States.

HEIGHT 3 to 4 inches high, spreading 3 feet and more; low, ground-hugging habit.

CULTURE Prefers moist, well-drained acid soil in shade or full sun. Propagated by cuttings and by division.

DESCRIPTION Broadleaf evergreen. Dark green, glossy, oval leaves form a low, dense, decorative ground cover, especially popular for shaded areas. Decorative, star-shaped, 1-inch blue flowers appear in early spring and continue for several months. A similar species, *Vinca major*, has slightly larger flowers. It is not so hardy, but is popular in the South and mild-winter areas.

LANDSCAPE USE Good weed-smothering ground cover, particularly in deep shade where other ground covers will not grow. Also suitable for planting in window boxes so the creeping stems can hang down the sides.

BOTANICAL NAME *Vitex agnus-castus*

COMMON NAME Chaste-tree

RANGE Zones 7–10. Native to the Mediterranean.

HEIGHT 10 to 20 feet high with equal spread; loose, spreading habit.

CULTURE Prefers moderately dry, fertile, well-drained soil in full sun. Enjoys seashore conditions. Propagated by cuttings.

DESCRIPTION Deciduous. Multiple trunks. Twigs and leaves are pleasantly aromatic. Leaves are divided fan-wise into five to seven leaflets and are dark green above and gray beneath. Fragrant, long-lasting spikes of lavender-blue flowers, 7 inches long, bloom August through October.

LANDSCAPE USE Good in a shrub border for late-summer flowering. Popular in hot climates because it is heat-resistant. North of zone 7, top growth may be killed to the ground in winter, but new growth with flowering stems will sprout in the spring.

Right: Flowering crabapple flaunts its pale pink blossoms above a border of azaleas planted beside this woodland path.

BOTANICAL NAME *Weigela florida*

COMMON NAME Weigela

RANGE Zones 5–8. Native to Japan.

HEIGHT 6 to 9 feet tall and 9 to 12 feet wide; spreading habit.

CULTURE Prefers well-drained loam soil in full sun. Tolerant to air pollution. Prune to retain compact shape. Propagated by cuttings.

DESCRIPTION Deciduous, dense, old-fashioned shrub. Grown primarily for its profuse show of reddish to rose-pink blossoms in May and June. Flowers are 1 1/4 inches long and grow in groups of three or four on short, grayish twigs. The oval-shaped leaves are light green and 2 to 4 inches long. No fall color.

LANDSCAPE USE Frequently used in shrub borders, groupings, massings, or foundation plantings. Resembles an azalea, but is later-flowering.

BOTANICAL NAME *Wisteria floribunda*

COMMON NAME Wisteria

RANGE Zones 4–9. Native to Japan.

HEIGHT Up to 30 feet; vine.

CULTURE Prefers well-drained, loamy garden soil in full sun. Propagated by seed.

DESCRIPTION Deciduous vine that can be shaped into a tree or shrub. Prune back stems that interfere with framework of desired form. The main stem will become a good-sized trunk. Provide good support and train developing stems to enhance desired shape. Bright green leaves are 12 to 16 inches long and are divided into fifteen to nineteen leaflets. Long, 18-inch clusters of fragrant violet to violet-blue flowers burst into bloom in April and May.

LANDSCAPE USE Excellent flowering vine. Good to train over arbors, along balconies, and the top of walls. There is a double-flowered form. A blue and white intertwined has an especially beautiful flowering effect.

Left: Dwarf boxwood creates a "parterre" garden where low hedges delineate planting beds.

CHAPTER FOUR

PLANT SELECTION GUIDE

THE FOLLOWING LISTS SHOULD BE HELPFUL in deciding which shrubs to choose for a particular purpose. Here you will find shrubs suitable for hedging, ground cover effects, vining habit, and a multitude of other purposes.

These lists are not absolute. Shrubs are versatile plants and part of the fun of growing them is to find uncommon uses. For example, almost every shrub can be trained into a hedge and some vining plants normally used to climb walls can also be trained to creep across the ground as a ground cover.

LOW SHRUBS FOR GROUND COVERS

Allamanda cathartica (Yellow Allamanda)
Ardisia japonica (Marlberry)
Calluna vulgaris (Scotch Heather)
Cotoneaster horizontalis (Rock Spray)
Gelsemium sempervirens (Carolina Jessamine)
Hedera helix (English Ivy)
Hypericum calycinum (St.-John's-wort)
Leucothoe fontanesiana (Drooping Leucothoe)
Lonicera japonica (Japanese Honeysuckle)
Parthenocissus quinquefolia (Virginia Creeper)
Potentilla fruticosa (Bush Cinquefoil)
Trachelospermum jasminoides (Star or Confederate Jasmine)

NARROWLEAF EVERGREENS

Chamaecyparis pisifera (False Cypress)
Juniperus horizontalis (Creeping Juniper)
Picea pungens nana (Dwarf Blue Spruce)
Pinus mugo (Mugo Pine)
Podocarpus macrophyllus (Yew Podocarpus)
Taxus cuspidata (Japanese Yew)
Tsuga canadensis 'Sargenti' (Weeping Hemlock)

VINES

Actinidia chinensis (Kiwi)
Allamanda cathartica (Yellow Allamanda)
Beaumontia grandiflora (Easter Lily Vine)
Bougainvillea spectabilis (Bougainvillea)
Celastrus scandens (American Bittersweet)
Clematis species and hybrids (Clematis)
Gelsemium sempervirens (Carolina Jessamine)
Hedera helix (English Ivy)
Lantana camara (Shrub Verbena)
Lonicera japonica (Japanese Honeysuckle)
Parthenocissus quinquefolia (Virginia Creeper)
Trachelospermum jasminoides (Star or Confederate Jasmine)
Wisteria floribunda (Wisteria)

SHRUBS TO GROW FROM SEED

Although most shrubs can be grown from seed, it is usually faster to propagate them from cuttings. The following kinds of shrubs are particularly easy to grow from seed, and they are reasonably fast-growing. Besides being inexpensive, growing shrubs from seed offers the chance of producing an unusual new variety since seed-grown shrubs often differ from the parent plant, as opposed to cuttings, which are identical.

Acer palmatum dissectum (Japanese Maple)
Aucuba japonica (Gold-dust Plant)
Azalea kaempferi (Kaempferi Azalea)
Azalea mollis (Mollis Azalea)
Berberis thunbergii atropurpurea (Japanese Barberry)
Buddleia davidii (Butterfly Bush)
Calluna vulgaris (Scotch Heather)
Camellia japonica (Camellia)
Campsis radicans (Trumpetcreeper; Trumpetvine; Hummingbird Vine)
Caryopteris x *clandonensis* (Blue-mist Shrub; Hybrid Bluebeard)
Ceanothus species (California Lilac)
Cistus ladanifer (Crimson-spot Rock-rose; Gum Rock-rose)
Clematis paniculata (Sweet Autumn Clematis)
Cornus florida (Flowering Dogwood)
Cornus kousa (Korean Dogwood)
Cotinus coggygria (Smoketree)
Cotoneaster horizontalis (Rock Spray Cotoneaster)
Cytisus scoparius (Scotch Broom)
Daphne species (Daphne)
Enkianthus campanulatus (Redvein Enkianthus)
Euonymus alata (Burning Bush; Winged Euonymus)
Fuchsia species and hybrids (Fuchsia)
Hamamelis species (Witch-hazels)
Hibiscus species (Hibiscus)
Ilex species (Hollies)
Kalmia latifolia (Mountain-laurel)
Kolkwitzia amabilis (Beautybush)
Lonicera species (Honeysuckle)
Paeonia suffruticosa (Tree Peony)
Parthenocissus quinquefolia (Virginia Creeper)
Picea species (Spruce)
Pinus species (Pines)

Pyracantha coccinea (Scarlet Firethorn)
Rhododendron species and hybrids (Rhododendrons and Azaleas)
Rosa species (Roses)
Skimmia japonica (Japanese Skimmia)
Syringa species (Lilacs)
Viburnum opulus sterile (European Snowball Bush)
Wisteria species (Wisteria)

SHRUBS FOR THE SEASHORE

Callistemon citrinus (Lemon Bottlebrush)
Ceanothus thyrsiflorus (California Lilac)
Cistus ladanifer (Crimson-spot Rock-rose)
Cytisus scoparius (Scotch Broom)
Hibiscus syriacus (Rose of Sharon)
Juniperus horizontalis (Creeping Juniper)
Myrica cerifera (Southern Wax-myrtle)
Nerium oleander (Oleander)
Pittosporum tobira (Japanese Pittosporum)
Raphiolepis indica (Indian Hawthorn)
Tamarix ramosissima (Tamarix)
Vitex agnus-castus (Chaste-tree)

BROADLEAF EVERGREENS

Abelia x *grandiflora* (Glossy Abelia)
Allamanda cathartica (Yellow Allamanda)
Ardisia japonica (Marlberry)
Aucuba japonica 'Variegata' (Gold-dust Plant)
Beaumontia grandiflora (Herald's-trumpet)
Brunfelsia calycina floribunda (Yesterday, Today, Tomorrow)
Buxus sempervirens (English Boxwood)
Calliandra haematocephala (Powderpuff Shrub)
Callistemon citrinus (Lemon Bottlebrush)
Camellia japonica (Camellia)
Carissa grandiflora (Natal-Plum)
Cotoneaster horizontalis (Rock Spray)
Euonymus japonicus (Japanese Euonymus)
Gardenia jasminoides (Gardenia)
Gelsemium sempervirens (Carolina Jessamine)
Hedera helix (English Ivy)
Hypericum calycinum (St.-John's-wort)
Ilex x *meservae* (Blue Holly)
Ilex verticillata (Winterberry)
Kalmia latifolia (Mountain-laurel)
Leucothoe fontanesiana (Drooping Leucothoe)
Ligustrum x *vicaryi* (Vicary Golden Privet)
Mahonia aquifolium (Oregon Holly-grape)
Mahonia bealei (Leatherleaf Mahonia)
Nerium oleander (Oleander)
Photinia x *fraseri* (Red Tips)
Pieris japonica (Japanese Andromeda)
Pittosporum tobira (Japanese Pittosporum)
Pyracantha coccinea (Scarlet Firethorn)
Raphiolepis indica (Indian Hawthorn)
Rhododendron species (Rhododendron)
Rhododendron (Azalea)
Skimmia japonica (Japanese Skimmia)
Trachelospermum jasminoides (Star or Confederate Jasmine)

Opposite page: Chinese snowball bush (*Viburnum macrocephalum*) is much larger flowered than the more common European snowball bush (*Viburnum opulus* 'sterile'), but is not reliably hardy north of Wilmington, Delaware.

SHRUBS FROM CUTTINGS

Where there is a preference between a softwood or hardwood cutting, it is given in parentheses.

Abelia x grandiflora (softwood)
Acer palmatum
Actinidia chinensis
Allamanda carthartica
Amelanchier arborea (softwood)
Aucuba japonica
Beaumontia grandiflora
Berberis thunbergii
Bougainvillea spectabilis
Brunfelsia calyana floribunda
Buddleia davidii (hardwood)

Buxus sempervirens (hardwood)
Calliandra haematocephala (hardwood)
Callicarpa japonica (softwood)
Callistemon citrinus
Calluna vulgaris (softwood)
Camellia japonica (softwood)
Campsis radicans (softwood)
Carissa grandiflora
Caryopteris x *clandonensis* (softwood)
Ceanothus thyrsiflorus
Celastrus scandens (softwood)
Cercis chinensis (semi-hardwood)
Chaenomeles speciosa (semi-hardwood)
Chamaecyparis pisifera
Cistus ladanifera
Clematis species
Cornus florida (softwood)
Cornus kousa (softwood)
Cornus mas (softwood)
Corus sericea (softwood)
Corylopsis glabrescens (softwood)
Cotinus coggygria (softwood)
Cotoneaster horizontalis (softwood)
Cytisus scoparius (hardwood)
Daphne x *burkwoodii* (semi-hardwood)
Deutzia gracilis (softwood)
Enkianthus campanulatus (softwood)
Escallonia exoniensis
Euonymus alata (softwood)
Euonymus japonicus
Exochorda racemosa (semi-hardwood)
Fatsia japonica (semi-hardwood)
Forsythia x *intermedia* (softwood)
Fothergilla gardenii (softwood)
Fuchsia hybrida (softwood)
Gardenia jasminoides (softwood)
Gelsemium sempervirens (hardwood)
Hamamelis mollis (semi-hardwood)
Hedera helix (softwood)
Hibiscus syriacus (hardwood)
Hydrangea macrophylla (softwood)
Hypericum calycinum (softwood)

Ilex x *meserveae*
Ilex verticillata (softwood)
Juniperus horizontalis (softwood, but difficult)
Kalmia latifolia
Kerria japonica
Kolkwitzia amabilis (softwood)
Lagerstroemia indica (softwood)
Lantana camara
Leucothoe fortanesiana
Ligustrum x *vicaryi*
Lonicera japonica
Magnolia stellata (softwood)
Myrica cerifera
Nandina domestica
Nerium oleander (softwood)
Osmanthus heterophyllus
Paeonia suffruticosa
Parthenocissus quinquefolia (softwood)
Philadelphus coronarius (softwood)
Photinia x *fraseri* (softwood)
Picea pungens
Pieris japonica
Pinus mugo
Pittosporum tobira (hardwood)
Podocarpus macrophyllus (hardwood)
Potentilla fruticosa (softwood)
Prunus glandulosa
Pyracantha coccinea (softwood)
Rhododendron (hardwood)
Salix discolor
Skimmia japonica
Spiraea x *vanhouttei* (softwood)
Syringa vulgaris (softwood)
Taxus cuspidata
Trachelospermum jasminoides (softwood)
Tsuga canadensis (difficult)
Viburnum opulus (softwood)
Vinca minor
Vitex agnus-castus (softwood)
Weigela florida (softwood)
Wisteria floribunda

Opposite page: Japanese cut-leaf maples, artistically pruned of lower branches, expose an exotic tracery of twisted trunks and sinuous branches, in the Japanese Garden of Swiss Pines, near Philadelphia, Pennsylvania.

TALL SHRUBS FOR SCREENING

Berberis thunbergii atropurpurea (Japanese Barberry)
Buxus sempervirens (English Boxwood)
Camellia japonica (Camellia)
Carissa grandiflora (Natal-Plum)
Ceanothus thyrsiflorus (California Lilac)
Chaenomeles speciosa (Flowering Quince)
Osmanthus heterophyllus (Holly Osmanthus)
Photinia x *fraseri* (Red Tips)
Pieris japonica (Japanese Andromeda)
Pittosporum tobira (Japanese Pittosporum)
Podocarpus macrophyllus (Yew Podocarpus)
Raphiolepis indica (Indian Hawthorn)
Rhododendron species (Rhododendon)
Taxus cuspidata (Japanese Yew)
Viburnum opulus sterile (European Snowball Bush)

AUTUMN FOLIAGE COLOR

Acer palmatum dissectum (Japanese Maple)
Amelanchier arborea (Serviceberry)
Berberis thunbergii atropurpurea (Japanese Barberry)
Callicarpa japonica (Japanese Beauty Berry)
Campsis radicans (Trumpetcreeper)
Cercis chinensis (Chinese Redbud)
Cornus species (Dogwood)
Corylopsis glabrescens (Fragrant Winterhazel)
Cotinus coggygria (Smoketree)
Enkianthus campanulatus (Redvein Enkianthus)
Euonymous alata (Burning Bush)
Fothergillia gardenii (Dwarf Fothergilla)
Hamamelis mollis (Chinese Witch-hazel)
Kerria japonica (Japanese Kerria)
Kolkwitzia amabilis (Beautybush)
Lagerstroemia indica (Crape-myrtle)
Magnolia stellata (Star Magnolia)
Nandina domestica (Heavenly-bamboo)
Parthenocissus quinquefolia (Virginia Creeper)
Spiraea x *vanhouttei* (Bridalwreath)
Viburnum opulus sterile (European Snowball Bush)

SHRUBS SUITABLE FOR LAYERING

Amelanchier arborea (Serviceberry)
Azalea (Azalea)
Berberis thunbergii (Japanese Barberry)
Bougainvillea spectabilis (Bougainvillea)
Chaenomeles speciosa (Flowering Quince)
Cornus sericea (Red-twig Dogwood)
Cotoneaster horizontalis (Rock-spray)
Cytisus scoparius (Scotch Broom)
Enkianthus campanulatus (Redvein Eukianthus)
Euonymus japonica (Japanese Euonymus)
Exochorda racemosa (Pearlbush)
Fothergilla gardenii (Dwarf Fothergilla)
Hamamelis mollis (Witch-hazel)
Ilex x *meserveae* (Blue Holly)
Ilex verticillata (Winterberry)
Juniperus horizontalis (Creeping Juniper)
Kalmia latifolia (Mountain Laurel)
Magnolia (Magnolia)
Philadelphus coronarius (Sweet Mock-orange)
Photinia x *fraseri* (Red Tips)
Pieris japonica (Andromeda)
Potentilla fruticosa (Bush Cinquefoil)
Pyracantha coccinea (Firethorn)
Raphiolepis indica (Indian Hawthorn)
Rhododendron (Rhododendron)
Syringa vulgaris (Lilac)
Viburnum opulus sterile (European Snowball Bush)

Right, top: Topiary hounds clipped out of Japanese yew at the Ladew Topiary Gardens, near Monkton, Maryland.

Right, bottom: Azaleas flank a stairway. Such severe pruning must be done after the plants have finished flowering, but before September, in order to give the plants sufficient time to set flower buds for the following season's bloom.

HEDGES

Abelia x *grandiflora* (Glossy Abelia)
Amelanchier arborea (Serviceberry)
Aucuba japonica 'Variegata' (Gold-dust Plant)
Berberis thunbergii atropurpurea (Japanese Barberry)
Buxus sempervirens (English Boxwod)
Camellia japonica (Camellia)
Callistemon citrinus (Bottlebrush)
Carissa grandiflora (Natal-plum)
Cercis chinensis (Chinese Redbud)
Cytisus scoparius (Scotch Broom)
Deutzia gracilis (Slender Deutzia)
Enkianthus campanulatus (Redvein Enkianthus)
Euonymus alata (Burning Bush)
Euonymus japonica (Japanese Euonymus)
Forsythia x *intermedia* (Forsythia)
Ilex meserveae (Blue Holly)
Kerria japonica (Japanese Kerria)
Kolkwitzia amabilis (Beautybush)
Lantana camara (Shrub Verbena)
Ligustrum x *vicaryi* (Vicary Golden Privet)
Nerium oleander (Oleander)
Osmanthus heterophyllus (Holly Osmanthus)
Photinia x *fraseri* (Red Tips)
Picea pungens nana (Dwarf Blue Spruce)
Podocarpus macrophyllus (Yew Podocarpus)
Poncirus trifoliata (Hardy-orange)
Raphiolepis indica (Indian Hawthorn)
Spirea x *vanhouttei* (Bridalwreath)

TOPIARY

Buxus sempervirens (English Boxwood)
Hedera helix (English Ivy)
Ligustrum x *vicaryi* (Vicary Golden Privet)
Podocarpus macrophyllus (Yew Podocarpus)
Taxus cuspidata (Japanese Yew)

ESPALIER

Beaumontia grandiflora (Herald's-trumpet)
Calliandra haematocephala (Powderpuff Shrub)
Callistemon citrinus (Lemon Bottlebrush)
Fuchsia hybrida (Fuchsia)
Podocarpus macrophyllus (Yew Podocarpus)
Pyracantha coccinea (Scarlet Firethorn)

SHOWY FRUITS AND BERRIES

Actinidia chinensis (Kiwi)
Amelanchier arborea (Serviceberry)
Ardisia japonica (Marlberry)
Aucuba japonica 'Variegata' (Gold-dust Plant)
Berberis thunbergii atropurpurea (Japanese Barberry)
Callicarpa japonica (Japanese Beauty Berry)
Carissa grandiflora (Natal-plum)
Celastrus scandens (American Bittersweet)
Chaenomeles speciosa (Flowering Quince)
Cornus species (Dogwood)
Cotoneaster horizontalis (Rock Spray)
Daphne x *burkwodii* (Burkwood Daphne)
Ilex x *meservae* (Blue Holly)
Ilex verticillata (Winterberry)
Kalmia latifolia (Mountain-laurel)
Myrica cerifera (Southern Wax-myrtle)
Nandina domestica (Heavenly-bamboo)
Pyracantha coccinea (Scarlet Firethorn)
Raphiolepis indica (Indian Hawthorn)
Skimmia japonica (Japanese Skimmia)
Viburnum opulus sterile (European Snowball Bush)

Opposite page: Wisteria is the favored vine for decorating the tops of walls. Here, in the garden at Dumbarton Oaks, in Washington, D.C., it contrasts beautifully with English ivy.

SHOWY FLOWERING

Abelia x *grandiflora* (Glossy Abelia)
Allamanda cathartica (Yellow Allamanda)
Beaumontia grandiflora (Herald's-trumpet)
Bougainvillea species (Bougainvillea)
Brunfelsia calycina floribunda (Yesterday, Today, Tommorrow)
Buddleia davidii (Butterfly Bush)
Calliandra haematocephala (Powderpuff Shrub)
Callistemon citrinus (Lemon Bottlebrush)
Calluna vulgaris (Scotch Heather)
Camellia japonica (Camellia)
Campsis radicans (Trumpetcreeper)
Caryopteris x *clandonensis* (Blue-mist shrub)
Ceanothus thyrsiflorus (California Lilac)
Cercis chinensis (Chinese Redbud)
Chaenomeles speciosa (Flowering Quince)
Cistus ladanifer (Crimson-spot Rock-rose)
Clematis species and hybrids (Clematis)
Cornus species (Dogwood)
Corylopsis glabrescens (Fragrant Winterhazel)
Cotinus coggygria (Smoketree)
Cytisus scoparius (Scotch Broom)
Daphne x *burkwoodii* (Burkwood Daphne)
Deutzia gracilis (Slender Deutzia)
Enkianthus campanulatus (Redvein Enkianthus)
Exochorda racemosa (Pearlbush)
Forsythia x *intermedia* (Forsythia)
Fothergilla gardenii (Dwarf Fothergilla)
Fuchsia hybrida (Hybrid Fuchsia)
Gardenia jasminoides (Gardenia)
Gelsemium sempervirens (Carolina Jessamine)
Hamamelis mollis (Chinese Witch-hazel)
Hibiscus syriacus (Rose of Sharon)
Hydrangea macrophylla (Hydrangea)
Hypericum calycinum (St.-John's-wort)
Kalmia latifolia (Mountain-laurel)
Kerria japonica (Japanese Kerria)
Kolkwitzia amabilis (Beautybush)
Lagerstroemia indica (Crape-myrtle)
Lantana camara (Shrub Verbena)
Leucothoe fontanesiana (Drooping Leucothoe)
Lonicera japonica (Japanese Honeysuckle)
Magnolia stellata (Star Magnolia)
Nandina domestica (Heavenly-bamboo)

Nerium oleander (Oleander)
Osmanthus heterophyllus (Holly Osmanthus)
Philadelphus coronarius (Sweet Mock-Orange)
Photinia x *fraseri* (Red Tips)
Pieris japonica (Japanese Andromeda)
Pittosporum tobira (Japanese Pittosporum)
Poncirus trifoliata (Hardy-orange)
Potentilla fruticosa (Bush Cinquefoil)
Prunus glandulosa 'Alboplena' (Flowering Almond)
Pyracantha coccinea (Scarlet Firethorn)
Raphiolepis indica (Indian Hawthorn)
Rhododendron species (Rhododendron)
Rhododendron (Azalea)
Skimmia japonica (Japanese Skimmia)
Spiraea x *vanhouttei* (Bridalwreath)
Syringa vulgaris (Lilac)
Tamarix ramosissima (Tamarix)
Trachelospermum jasminoides (Star or Confederate Jasmine)
Viburnum opulus sterile (European Snowball Bush)
Vitex agnus-castus (Chaste-tree)
Weigela florida (Weigela)
Wisteria floribunda (Wisteria)

HARDINESS ZONE CHART

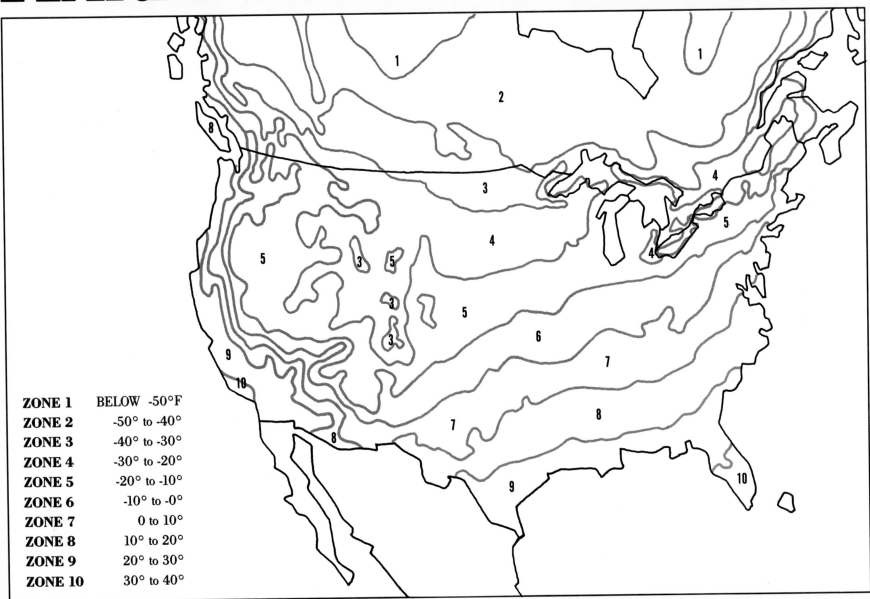

ZONE 1	BELOW -50°F
ZONE 2	-50° to -40°
ZONE 3	-40° to -30°
ZONE 4	-30° to -20°
ZONE 5	-20° to -10°
ZONE 6	-10° to -0°
ZONE 7	0 to 10°
ZONE 8	10° to 20°
ZONE 9	20° to 30°
ZONE 10	30° to 40°

SHRUB FLOWERING CHART

		January	February	March	April	May	June	July	August	September	October	November	December
Abelia x *grandiflora*	(Glossy Abelia)						■	■	■	■			
Acer palmatum dissectum	(Japanese Maple)			E V E R G R E E N									
Actinidia chinensis	(Kiwi)									■	■		
Allamanda cathartica 'Williamsi'	(Yellow Allamanda)						■	■	■	■			
Amelanchier arborea	(Serviceberry)			■	■								
Ardisia japonica	(Marlberry; Japanese Ardisia)	■	■	■	■								
Aucuba japonica 'Variegata'	(Gold-dust Plant)			E V E R G R E E N									
Beaumontia grandiflora	(Herald's-trumpet)					■							
Berberis thunbergii atropurpurea	(Japanese Barberry)			E V E R G R E E N									
Bougainvillea spectabilis	(Bougainvillea)	■			■	■	■			■	■	■	■
Brunfelsia calycina floribunda	(Yesterday, Today, Tomorrow)				■	■							
Buddleia davidii	(Butterfly Bush)							■	■				
Buxus sempervirens	(English Boxwood)			E V E R G R E E N									
Calliandra haematocephala	(Powderpuff Shrub)			■	■								
Callicarpa japonica	(Japanese Beauty Berry)									■	■		
Callistemon citrinus	(Lemon Bottlebrush)				■	■							
Calluna vulgaris	(Scotch Heather)								■	■			
Camellia japonica	(Camellia)	■	■	■									
Campsis radicans	(Trumpetcreeper)							■	■				
Carissa grandiflora	(Natal-Plum)	■	■	■	■	■	■	■	■	■	■	■	■
Caryopteris x *clandonensis*	(Blue-mist shrub; Bluebeard)								■	■			
Ceanothus thyrsiflorus	(California Lilac)			■	■								
Celastrus scandens	(American Bittersweet)									■	■		
Cercis chinensis	(Chinese Redbud)				■	■							

SHRUB FLOWERING CHART

		Jan	Feb	Mar	Apr	May	Jun	Jul	Aug	Sep	Oct	Nov	Dec
Chaenomeles speciosa	(Flowering Quince)			▓	▓								
Chamaceyparis pisifera	(False Cypress)			E V E R G R E E N									
Cistus ladanifer	(Crimson-spot Rock-rose)						▓	▓	▓	▓			
Clematis species and hybrids	(Clematis)					▓	▓	▓	▓				
Cornus florida	(Flowering Dogwood)					▓							
Cornus kousa	(Korean Dogwood)						▓						
Cornus mas	(Cornelian-cherry)				▓								
Cornus sericea	(Red-twig Dogwood)	▓	▓	▓								▓	▓
Corylopsis glabrescens	(Fragrant Winterhazel)			▓	▓								
Cotinus coggygria	(Smoketree)							▓	▓				
Cotoneaster horizontalis	(Rock Spray)										▓	▓	▓
Cytisus scoparius	(Scotch Broom)				▓	▓							
Daphne x *burkwoodii*	(Burkwood Daphne)					▓							
Deutzia gracilis	(Slender Deutzia)					▓							
Enkianthus campanulatus	(Redvein Enkianthus)					▓							
Escallonia exoniensis	(Escallonia)						▓	▓	▓	▓			
Euonymus alata	(Burning Bush)			E V E R G R E E N									
Euonymus japonicus	(Japanese Euonymus)			E V E R G R E E N									
Exochorda racemosa	(Pearlbush)					▓							
Fatsia japonica	(Japanese Aralia)			E V E R G R E E N									
Forsythia x *intermedia*	(Forsythia)			▓	▓								
Fothergilla gardenii	(Dwarf Fothergilla)				▓	▓							
Fuchsia hybrida	(Hybrid Fuchsia)						▓	▓	▓	▓	▓		
Gardenia jasminoides	(Gardenia; Cape-jasmine)			▓	▓								

SHRUB FLOWERING CHART

		January	February	March	April	May	June	July	August	September	October	November	December
Gelsemium sempervirens	(Carolina Jessamine)			▓	▓								
Hamamelis mollis	(Chinese Witch-hazel)		▓	▓									
Hedera helix	(English Ivy)					E V E R G R E E N							
Hibiscus syriacus	(Rose of Sharon; Shrub Althea)								▓	▓			
Hydrangea macrophylla	(Hydrangea)						▓	▓					
Hypericum calycinum	(St.-John's-wort)						▓						
Ilex x *meserveae*	(Blue Holly; Meserve Hybrids)	▓	▓	▓									▓
Ilex verticillata	(Winterberry)										▓	▓	▓
Juniperus horizontalis	(Creeping Juniper)					E V E R G R E E N							
Kalmia latifolia	(Mountain-laurel)						▓						
Kerria japonica	(Japanese Kerria)					▓							
Kolkwitzia amabilis	(Beauty Bush)												
Lagerstroemia indica	(Crape-myrtle)							▓	▓	▓			
Lantana camara	(Shrub Verbena)						▓	▓	▓	▓			
Leucothoe fontanesiana	(Drooping Leucothoe)					▓							
Ligustrum x *vicaryi*	(Vicary Golden Privet)					E V E R G R E E N							
Lonicera japonica 'Halliana'	(Japanese Honeysuckle)						▓	▓					
Magnolia stellata	(Star Magnolia)			▓									
Myrica cerifera	(Southern Wax-myrtle)			▓									
Nandina domestica	(Heavenly-bamboo; Nandina)	▓									▓	▓	
Nerium oleander	(Oleander)						▓	▓	▓				
Osmanthus heterophyllus	(Holly Osmanthus)					E V E R G R E E N							
Paeonia suffruticosa	(Tree Peony)					▓							
Parthenocissus quinquefolia	(Virginia Creeper)					E V E R G R E E N							

SHRUB FLOWERING CHART

Botanical Name	Common Name	January	February	March	April	May	June	July	August	September	October	November	December
Philadelphus coronarius	(Sweet Mock-orange)						■						
Photinia x *fraseri*	(Fraser Photinia; Red Tips)					■							
Picea pungens nana	(Dwarf Blue Spruce)			E	V	E	R	G	R	E	E	N	
Pieris japonica	(Japanese Andromeda)			■	■								
Pinus mugo	(Mugo Pine)			E	V	E	R	G	R	E	E	N	
Pittosporum tobira	(Japanese Pittosporum)			E	V	E	R	G	R	E	E	N	
Podocarpus macrophyllus	(Yew Podocarpus)			E	V	E	R	G	R	E	E	N	
Poncirus trifoliata	(Hardy-orange)										■		
Potentilla fruticosa	(Bush Cinquefoil)					■	■	■	■				
Prunus glandulosa 'Alboplena'	(Flowering Almond)				■								
Pyracantha coccinea	(Scarlet Firethorn)										■	■	■
Raphiolepis indica	(Indian Hawthorn)			■						■			
Rhododendron species (Azalea)	(Azalea)				■	■							
Salix discolor	(Pussy Willow)			■									
Skimmia japonica	(Japanese Skimmia)										■	■	■
Spiraea x *vanhouttei*	(Bridalwreath; Vanhoutte Spirea)					■	■						
Syringa vulgaris	(Lilac)					■							
Tamarix ramosissima	(Tamarix)					■							
Taxus cuspidata	(Japanese Yew)			E	V	E	R	G	R	E	E	N	
Trachelospermum jasminoides	(Star or Confederate Jasmine)								■	■	■		
Tsuga canadensis 'Sargentii'	(Weeping Hemlock)			E	V	E	R	G	R	E	E	N	
Viburnum opulus sterile	(European Snowball Bush)					■	■						
Vinca minor	(Periwinkle; Myrtle)			■	■	■							
Vitex agnus-castus	(Chaste-tree)							■					

SHRUB FLOWERING CHART

	January	February	March	April	May	June	July	August	September	October	November	December
Weigela florida (Weigela)						▓						
Wisteria floribunda (Wisteria)					▓	▓						

THE FOLLOWING NURSERIES SPECIALIZE IN selling shrubs by mail. Before making inquiries, request a copy of their catalog.

Beaver Creek Nursery
7526 Pelleaux Road
Knoxville, TN 37938
Specializes in collector's trees and shrubs.
Catalog $1.00.

The Bovees Nursery
1737 S.W. Coronado
Portland, OR 97219
Specializes in species and hybrid rhododendrons.
Catalog $2.00.

W. Atlee Burpee Company
300 Park Avenue
Warminster, PA 18974
Offers plants, seeds, books, supplies, tools, and bulbs.
Catalog free.

Carroll Gardens
P.O. Box 310
444 East Main Street
Westminster, MD 21157
Large selection including hollies, yews, viburnums, and much more.
Catalog $2.00.

Gardens of the Blue Ridge
P. O. Box 10
U.S. 221 N.
Pineola, NC 28662
Good selection of native shrubs.
Catalog $2.00.

Girard Nurseries
P.O. Box 428
6801 North Ridge (US 20)
Geneva, OH 44041
Broad selection of flowering shrubs, dwarf conifers rhododendrons, azaleas, and hollies.
Catalog free.

Gurney Seed & Nursery Company
2nd and Capital
Yankton, SC 57078
Offers broad selection of plants and seeds.
Catalog free.

Hall Rhododendrons
1280 Quince Drive
Junction City, OR 97448
Offers broad selection of species and hybrid rhododendrons and azaleas.
Catalog $1.00.

Hortico, Inc.
723 Robson Rd., R.R. 1
Waterdown, ON, Canada
L0R2H0
Specializes in a broad selection of garden perennials along with ornamental trees, shrubs, ferns, wildflowers, and conifers.
Catalog free.

Krider Nurseries
P. O. Box 29
Middlebury, IN 46540
Broad selection of fruit trees, berries, ornamental trees, shrubs, and roses.
Catalog free.

Lawyer Nursery, Inc.
950 Highway 200 West
Plains, MT 59859
Many types of ornamental trees, fruit and nut trees, rootstock for fruit trees, conifers, and shrubs.
Catalog free.

Musser Forests, Inc.
P. O. Box 340
Route 119 North
Indiana, PA 15710-0340
Supplies trees, shrubs, and ground covers.
Catalog free.

Spring Hill Nurseries Co.
P. O. Box 1758
Peoria, IL 61656
Broad selection of perennials, flowering shrubs, ground covers.
Catalog free.

Wayside Gardens
P. O. Box 1
Hodges, SC 29695-0001
Offers ornamental trees and shrubs, perennials, and roses.
Catalog $1.00.

INDEX OF BOTANICAL AND COMMON NAMES